Africa's Transition from Colonisation to Independence and Decolonisation:

Joseph Conrad's *Heart of Darkness*,

Chinua Achebe's *Things Fall Apart*,

and

Moses Isegawa's *Abyssinian Chronicles*

Ulrich Pallua

AFRICA'S TRANSITION FROM COLONISATION TO
INDEPENDENCE AND DECOLONISATION:

Joseph Conrad's *Heart of Darkness*,
Chinua Achebe's *Things Fall Apart*,
and
Moses Isegawa's *Abyssinian Chronicles*

ibidem-Verlag
Stuttgart

Bibliografische Information Der Deutschen Bibliothek

Die Deutsche Bibliothek verzeichnet diese Publikation in der Deutschen Nationalbibliografie; detaillierte bibliografische Daten sind im Internet über <http://dnb.ddb.de> abrufbar.

∞

Gedruckt auf alterungsbeständigem, säurefreien Papier
Printed on acid-free paper

ISBN: 3-89821-353-6
© *ibidem*-Verlag
Stuttgart 2004
Alle Rechte vorbehalten

Das Werk einschließlich aller seiner Teile ist urheberrechtlich geschützt. Jede Verwertung außerhalb der engen Grenzen des Urheberrechtsgesetzes ist ohne Zustimmung des Verlages unzulässig und strafbar. Dies gilt insbesondere für Vervielfältigungen, Übersetzungen, Mikroverfilmungen und elektronische Speicherformen sowie die Einspeicherung und Verarbeitung in elektronischen Systemen.

Printed in Germany

Table of Contents

I.	**Introduction**	7
II.	**From Colonialism to Independence and Decolonisation**	
II.1.	Imperialistic Colonizer: Imperialism and Capitalism from the Metropolis	9
II.2.	Dominated Colonized: Redefining Blackness	
II.2.1.	The Creation of a "New" Language: "english"	11
II.3.	Violence of Postcolonial Independence	
II.3.1.	Decolonisation and its New Identity: Back to the Metropolis	16
III.	***Heart of Darkness***	
III.1.	Life and Works of Joseph Conrad	21
III.2.	Introduction to *Heart of Darkness*	23
III.3.	Congo Free State: Early History	24
III.4.	Conrad's Personal Experience in the Congo	25
III.5.	Conrad as a Child of the 19th Century	
III.5.1.	Racism and Reactions	28
III.6.	The Narrator and Conrad's Narrative Technique	30
III.7.	The Notion of Work/Language Within the Dream-Like Journey	34
III.8.	Marlow's Discovery: A Choice of Nightmares	39
III.9.	Kurtz's Unspeakable Rites	42
III.10.	Kurtz as the Harbinger of Light	45
III.11.	Reactions to Conrad's Intention of *Heart of Darkness*	47

IV.	***Things Fall Apart***	
IV.1.	The Life and Works of Chinua Achebe	51
IV.2.	Introduction to *Things Fall Apart*	53
IV.3.	Igbo History from 1860 to 1900	53
IV.4.	The Igboland and its Inhabitants	55
IV.5.	Achebe's Style and Language	58
IV.6.	Okonkwo: Society's Offspring and Lonely Wrestler	60
IV.7.	The Second Coming	62
IV.8.	The Female Vein: Okonkwo's Manliness and Refusal of His Feminine Side	64
IV.9.	The Personal Destiny: "Chi"	67
IV.10.	The Missionaries and the District Commissioner's Descent	69
V.	***Abyssinian Chronicles***	
V.1.	Life and Works of Moses Isegawa	73
V.2.	Introduction to *Abyssinian Chronicles*	73
V.3.	History of Uganda in the Second Half of the 20th Century	75
V.4.	Isegawa's Style and Language	77
V.5. V.5.1.	Post-Independent Search of Identity Woman and Religion	78
V.6.	White Religion as a Futile Attempt to Lessen Colonial Impact	83
V.7.	Amin's Heritage	86
V.8.	Back to the Imperial Metropolis	88
VI.	Conclusion	91
Bibliography		97

I. Introduction

The aim of this thesis is to visualize Africa from three different points of view; namely, to describe the image of Africa at three different stages of history. With reference to Africa's political background, from the 19th to the 20th century, Joseph Conrad, the coloniser, Chinua Achebe, the colonised, and Moses Isegawa, the decolonised, tell the story of the black continent and its development from colonisation to independence and decolonisation. Furthermore, this development epitomizes the 'heart of darkness' whose laws and characteristics have changed throughout the centuries. This concept of the 'dark heart' of the European colonisers forms the basis of the theoretical chapter about colonisation, independence and decolonisation. **Imperialism** and **capitalism** in the 'Metropolis' of the European coloniser were the driving forces behind the imperialistic enterprise and as a result, played a decisive role in invading and exploiting the African continent. *Heart of Darkness* by Joseph Conrad represents a starting point for the exploration of the African continent. Based on the political background in the Congo Free State, I will try to discover his technique and mode of depicting his personal experience in the Congo reflected in *Heart of Darkness*. As a matter of fact, Conrad was mostly criticised as being a racist because of his presentation of the African natives and their customs. Together with the insight into the real 'heart of darkness,' that of Kurtz and all the other 'harbingers of light,' Marlow's experience of the 'lie' will become clear. Kurtz, as the representative of the colonial 'Metropolis,' will take us to the point where it is up to the reader to decide whether the reactions to Joseph Conrad's first novel of the 20th century are justified or represent another step in the direction of redefining blackness. **Independence** marks a further step in the development towards a new identity of the black continent. The dominated colonised tries to redefine blackness, among many other things, through the creation of a 'new language,' namely, 'english.' Chinua Achebe with *Things Fall Apart* portrays a picture of the Igbo people in Nigeria before and after the arrival of the white missionaries. Once again, based on the political situation of the Igbos from 1860 to 1900, my thesis will visualise Achebe's language in depicting the descent of the 'white locusts' on African reality. Thus, the so-called 'Second Coming' highlights the principle of the female vein of the Igbo tribe, which brings about the tragic fall of the main character Okonkwo, and his cultural background in general. As a lonely wrestler and destined by his 'chi' to be the opposing force towards the white invasion, he is doomed to die. Giving the reader a picture of the circumstances of the white ignorance when getting in contact with the African 'counterpart' means defining the concept of the clash of cultures from the point of view of the dominated colonised. The violence of postcolonial independence introduces the concept of **decolonisation**, and at the same time the last stage of history of Africa presented in the thesis. The conception of a 'new identity' means the return of the decolonised African to the 'Metropolis' of white imperialism, which is still the centre of racism and prejudices. Moses Isegawa with his first novel *Abyssinian Chronicles* tries to reappraise the history of Uganda in the second half of the 20th century. Furthermore, he uses his language, his new 'english,' linguistically speaking, to name his personality and that of his fellow Africans. With reference to the post-independent search of identity, he stresses the significance of the notion of woman and religion for the rediscovery of Africa's self. The political situation in Uganda from 1960 onward dominates the bulk of the book and illustrates the atrocious system of Idi Amin. As a result, the aftermath of the tyranny proves to be even more appalling as the main protagonist of the book, Mugezi, is confronted with the regime on the national and the domestic scale. His mother embodies the colonial aggressor and exploiter of the African consciousness; consequently, the return to the 'Metropolis' and the problems with the female 'aspect' in general signify the lust for vengeance of the black man. In order to find one's identity or rather to discover a new one, it is necessary to fight against the oppression of the whites and the common feeling of inferiority among black people. This thought will link up to the conclusion where the attempt will be made to compare the three different works written at three different stages of history, and to show African reality from three different points of view. The comparison of these books offers an insight into the European and African history as well as a solution in the direction of the problem of 'whiteness' and 'blackness.'

II. From Colonisation to Independence and Decolonisation
II.1. Imperialistic Colonizer: Imperialism and Capitalism from the Metropolis

For the discussion of outstanding writers such as Joseph Conrad, Chinua Achebe and Moses Isegawa it is of vital importance to define the imperial situation of the 19th and 20th century in order to be able to comprehend their works. First and foremost, colonialism avoids any reference to the people who had already been living in the colonies; moreover, the definition refers only to the colonizers as such. Hence it evacuates the word 'colonialism' of any implication of an encounter between peoples, or of conquest and domination. There is no reference to the fact that the colonizers invaded and destroyed already existing cultures and domains. Therefore, "colonialism can be defined as the conquest and control of other people's land and goods."[1] The colonizers penetrated into the unknown and tried to define the 'other' by trying to identify them according to Victorian values. Capitalism was the dominating feature of the 19th century and was one of the main reasons for colonialism or rather imperialism: "capitalism is the distinguishing feature between colonialism and imperialism."[2] Therefore, imperialism had its centre in the metropolis of the so-called motherland, and "the granting of political independence signals the end of the empire, the collapse of imperialism. However, if imperialism is primarily an economic system of penetration and control of markets, then political changes do not basically affect it."[3] The metropolis impersonates the flow of money and power, which includes the active colonizers as cogs in the 'monster' imperialism, which pretends to bring the light of civilisation to the cannibals. Nevertheless, the dangers that the autonomy of these 'messengers' posed for bureaucratic objectives were obvious because they were "the puppet of an imperial destiny... puppet and puppeteer, instrument through which Britain realises its imperial destiny and initiating agent who conceptualises that destiny for Britain."[4] This is illustrated by the gap between the bureaucratic aim of the metropolis and its rulers, which is the exploitation of other cultures for their own

---

[1] Ania Loomba, *Colonialism/Postcolonialism* (London and NewYork: Routledge, 1998) 2.
[2] Ibid. 5.
[3] Ibid. 6.
[4] Daniel Bivona, *British Imperial Literature, 1870-1940. Writing and the Administration of Empire* (Cambridge: Cambridge UP, 1998) 104.

benefit, and the personal aspirations and intentions after the encounter with the African population. The imperial colonizer is the "company's man's dream of autonomous agency, a projection of a company operative so independent of bureaucratic control that he fulfils the prime function of the company – making profit – from a position of almost miraculous independence of its authority."[5] Thus, the whole process of civilizing a nation is seen as active work, which offers a possibility to be able to remain sane in the surroundings of the absolute abyss for the white man. Especially Conrad's *Heart of Darkness* visualizes the difference of the noble and sham Kurtz and all the 'missionaries' with their material aspirations. They despise him because of his success and possession of a moral imperative. The imperial character is in danger of "abandoning Company discipline, but he does so while ostensibly distancing himself from the Company men who accompany him upriver and from the discipline of the profit motive which controls the Company."[6] This capitalistic aspect of the company 'Europe' is condemned together with the brutal inefficiency of the European imperialism.

Capitalism as the prime feature of imperialism was identified as cannibalism that devours all the noble instincts in the human being. It is the "sheer brutality of the profit motive as a measure of human affairs and the profound irrationability of a system that must perforce devour itself"[7] and dehumanises the world of the 'other.' The colonizers enriched themselves by exploitation and "primitive accumulation." (Marx quoted in Phillips: 1998, 186) "The colonial capitalist was the vampire who gave life to the cannibal elite that ruled at home, with the aid of respectable forms."[8] The economic man was obsessed with his profit and in achieving this he did not care about the others who experienced his lust for money, his 'cannibalistic' tendencies, and his blind will of destruction. "In *Heart of Darkness*, capitalist anthropology is shown as necessarily tied to the obscenity of capitalist anthropophagy...and Marlow sees Kurtz as the irrational, cannibalistic principle of colonial expansionism, the corporeal symbol of an utterly amoral desire to incorporate all within the province of exploitation."[9] The process of colonisation implied the seemingly justifiable attitude

---

[5] Ibid. 106.
[6] Ibid. 109.
[7] Jerry Phillips, "Cannibalism qua capitalism: the Metaphorics of Accumulation in Marx, Conrad, Shakespeare, and Marlow," *Cannibalism and the Colonial World*, eds. Francis Baker, Peter Hulme, and Margaret Iversen (Cambridge: Cambridge UP, 1998) 185.
[8] Ibid. 186.
[9] Ibid. 188-9.

of the colonizers of imagining themselves "as doing God's work on earth...the colonial subject could only elevate himself by denigrating other human beings, who then become simply 'other.'"[10] The colonizer considered himself to have the right and obligation to civilize the population of the African continent and in the process highlighted the difference between whiteness and blackness. Similarly, he introduced the terms civilization and cannibalism; it was the "white man's burden"[11] to go and risk his life for the black people. Capitalist interests and ignorance were to doom the future of the black people because the

> Proletarian white supremacism is a (false) idol formed out of the raw materials of desire and hate, envy and enmity, nostalgia and estrangement, which combine in the ideological crucible of industrial discipline...the state of nature is typically what political economy claims to negate: beastliness is the primitive truth of capitalist discipline as moral progress, it is the truth of man labouring to transcend nature.[12]

II.2. Dominated Colonized: Redefining Blackness
II.2.1. The Creation of a "New" Language: "english"

James Balfour said in his speech to the House of Commons in 1910 that England exports "our very best to these countries," (Balfour quoted in Said: 1978, 33) namely the colonies. This means that the colonizers and the so-called motherland knew what was good for the colonies better than they could possibly know themselves. The Westerners were destined to dominate and the 'others' were to be dominated. Edward W. Said in his book *Orientalism* claims that Orientals[13] and colonized people in general are "devoid of energy and initiative, much given to intrigue, cunning and unkindness to animals...in everything oppose the clarity, directness, and nobility of the Anglo-Saxon race."[14] Besides, the colonizer was noble, respectful and grand whereas the colonized was depraved, irrational, different, and child- and devil-like. The white invader did not know anything about blackness and the colonized peoples'

---
[10] Ibid. 190.
[11] Rudyard Kipling, *White Man's Burden*, 1899.
[12] Phillips, *Cannibalism and the Colonial World* 193-4.
[13] With Orientals Said means the people from the East, especially from the Orient (India, Pakistan, Arabia, ...), but the Africans are included in the colonised peoples in general.
[14] Edward W. Said, *Orientalism* (New York: Vintage Books, 1978) 38-9.

customs and culture; what did it mean to be black? Why was black different from white? Blackness was considered inferior and therefore, it was meant to be extinguished because it was 'different' and not illegible for the white race. Cromer reminds us that "certain men can be singled out as the subject for proper study." (Cromer quoted in Said: 1978, 45) That is exactly what Achebe did with Okonkwo in *Things Fall Apart* because he chose an individual from the tribe of the Igbos and depicted their customs and culture through Okonkwo's tragic experience of the head-on collision with the white missionaries. The colonial power was unleashed upon the colonized and descended on Africa like locusts; moreover, they destroyed the indigenous culture of the inhabitants by ignoring the fact that there had existed a culture beforehand. The colonizers polarized the two different worlds and divided them into 'us' and 'them.' Beyond any doubt, "imaginative geography and history help the mind to intensify its own sense of itself by dramatizing the distance and difference between what is close to it and what is far away."[15] The African tribe experienced the coming of the white messenger, and at the same time the Africans were confronted with the white imperative, "a white middle-class Westerner believes it his human prerogative not only to manage the non-white world but also to own it, just because by definition 'it' is not quite as human as 'we' are."[16] Frantz Fanon states in *Black Skin, White Masks*, "the black man has two dimensions. One with his fellows, the other with the white man. A Negro behaves differently with a white man and with another Negro. That this self-division is a direct result of colonialist subjugation is beyond question."[17] Once again, the gap between the two cultures is seen from the points of view of the colonizer and the colonized. Colonialism has widened the rift by forcing the colonies into submission, which means that the colonies were forced to ignore their own language and customs and accept the foreigner's culture as their own. Fanon calls it the "inferiority complex."[18] The black man had a historical past, a past which had been vital and existing, but which was not respected by the blindfolded white imperialist.

Colonial domination manages to disrupt the actual life of the conquered people by believing in the non-existence of the oppressed situation of the "Wretched of the

---

[15] Ibid. 55.
[16] Ibid. 108.
[17] Frantz Fanon, *Black Skin, White Masks*, trans. Charles Lam Markmann (New York: Groove Press, 1967) 17.
[18] Ibid. 18.

Earth."[19] The colonizer forces the colonized to admit the "unreality of his nation...and the confused and imperfect character of his own biological structure...Colonial exploitation, poverty and endemic famine drive the native more and more to open, organized revolt. The necessity for an open and decisive breach is formed progressively and imperceptibly, and comes to be felt by the great majority of the people."[20] The natives are driven to open revolt because they are humiliated and therefore, stripped of their pride and honour; as a result, a possible option is to attack the colonizer and his system of rules and imperatives. The need for national consciousness among Africans is one of the main aims of the future but to successfully fulfil that task, the colonized, psychologically speaking, have to free themselves from their inferiority complex, which will "give them an international dimension."[21]

In order to make people aware of the existence of the African reality, for example, many post-colonial writers have written their books in different 'englishes,' namely the English of the "peripheries."[22] The black writer has been determined to be led into the white world, but at the same time he has always stressed his origins with a certain style of language. This includes the creation of a language "which will allow them to express their sense of 'Otherness'. Landscape, flora and fauna, seasons, climatic conditions are formally distinguished from the place of origin as home/colony, Europe/New World, Europe/Antipodes, and so on."[23] In relation to the political and social history of each country, the language can be read as a source of important images of national identity. The African writer still has his own response to the white world, and he has used English, whether "it supplanted the writer's mother tongue or simply offered an alternative medium which guaranteed a wider readership; its use caused a disjunction between the apprehension of, and communication about, the world."[24] The English language is used as a medium to reach people all over the world; consequently, this "appropriation and reconstitution of the language of the centre, the process of capturing and remoulding the language to new usages, makes a

---

[19] Frantz Fanon, *The Wretched of the Earth* (London: Penguin Books, 1963)
[20] Ibid. 190-2.
[21] Ibid. 199.
[22] Bill Ashcroft, Gareth Griffiths, and Helen Tiffin, *The Empire Writes Back. Theory and Practice in Post-Colonial Literatures* (London and New York: Routledge, 1989) 8. it refers to the eurocentric view of the colonizers who believed the colonies to be at the fringe in contrast to the centre of the metropolis.
[23] Ibid. 11.
[24] Ibid. 25.

separation from the site of colonial privilege."[25] This process includes the influence of the vernacular language, local language, and other englishes. It constructs difference, separation, and absence from the metropolis and signals a dismantling of the imperialist centralism. It creates difference but also sameness that allows the understanding of that kind of english which carries the cross-cultural feature of black identity. In the process of becoming a separate kind of language, english stresses its opposition to the centre and continuously questions the authority of the metropolis and the 'mother-culture.' Post-colonial works attempt to liberate 'themselves' from the distorted image created by the imperialist colonizer and to state their own appropriation of post-colonial reality. Strategies of appropriation state the authenticity of the 'colonized' texts, of the "reality of the world at the fringe" that has been producing a new mode of viewing imperialistic and colonial subjugation. All the englishes contribute to the enrichment of English literature and language, which in turn profits to a great extent from this multifocal relationship. "The central issue of a literary work is the strategic value of its content and the effectiveness of its intervention in the struggle to liberate African societies from economic injustice, social backwardness, and political reaction."[26] Ngugi wa Thiong'o has even gone a step further and has enlarged the African element in his novels by writing them in his mother tongue, which implies not writing for an elite but for his own people.

Certain features used by the black writer to 'alienate' the English language are the distinctive use of allegory, irony, magic realism and discontinuous narratives. "The prevalence of irony emphasises the importance of the language-place disjunction in the construction of post-colonial realities."[27] A lot of writers have rewritten works from colonial Britain in order to redefine values in post-colonial terms by reinterpreting the philosophical assumptions on which the old order was based or is still based. Ashcroft splendidly describes this process when he says that post-colonial writings "replace a temporal lineality with a spatial plurality."[28] The strategies, which such writing employs to maintain distance and otherness, are parenthetic translation of individual words, such as *obi* (hut); obi is established as a cultural sign. "The retention of the Igbo word perpetuates the metonymic function of the cross-cultural

---

[25] Ibid. 38.
[26] Ibid. 130.
[27] Ibid. 28.
[28] Ibid. 36.

text by allowing the word to stand for the latent presence of Igbo culture."[29] Untranslated words signify an even further gap between the cultures, and force the reader into an engagement with the culture. The fact that the words remain untranslated signals otherness and difference within the post-colonial text. "The choice of leaving words untranslated in post-colonial texts is a political act, because while translation is not inadmissible in itself, glossing gives the untranslated word, and thus the 'receptor' culture, the higher status."[30] Another technique is the creation of an "interlanguage" that "reveals that the utterances of a second-language learner are not deviant forms or mistakes, but rather a part of a separate but genuine linguistic system."[31] To make the dialect more accessible, code switching is used to install distinctiveness throughout the text, and to clarify the question of identity, which is one of the prime targets of post-colonial literature. The oral culture and the use of proverbs further underline the existing uniqueness of the African culture when the protagonists of the book rely on proverbs to base their existence on traditional values. The oral culture enriches the picture of African society because the reader realises the immense potential of the indigenous culture before ignorance denied its reality. Ashcroft concludes,

> literatures…reveal some of the most subtle examples of those processes such as code-switching, by which post-European cultures make english 'bear the burden' of an experience for which the terms of the inherited language do not seem appropriate. Such strategies…enable the construction of a distinctive social world.[32]

---

[29] Ibid. 62.
[30] Ibid. 66.
[31] Ibid. 68.
[32] Ibid. 75.

II.3. Violence of Post-Colonial Independence
II.3.1. Decolonisation and its New Identity: Back to the Metropolis

Decolonisation restructures the position of both colonizer and colonized because it spoils the old hierarchy. Therefore, the colonized first have to liberate themselves from the grip of the colonial power because its violence is omnipresent as "terrorism stands as the violence of decolonisation gone global."[33] In order to gain independence the old structure is torn down with the help of violence: "true decolonisation is something much more radical than the reversal of position and the replacement of rulers; decolonisation is the uprooting of the system as a whole, the supplanting of the political, existential, and corporeal reality created by colonisation."[34] The process of decolonisation threatens reality as a whole because it disrupts history, and therefore opens a gap, which has to be bridged in order to create a new reality. The aftermath of independence is characterised by chaos, loss of identity and confusion. The problem of independence includes disorder and oppression, military coup and dictatorship. Human rights were neglected and violated, and instability was commonplace. Although the former colonies had got rid of their masters, post-colonial reality was dominated by military rule and dictators such as Idi Amin, who terrorized the population of Uganda as its ruler from 1971 to 1979, and who brutally forced out the Indian population of the country and exterminated his political opposition. According to Raymond F. Betts, "imperialism and colonialism as ideologies justifying policies and institutions designed to ensure economic advantage through imposed political control are henceforth historical phenomena. In this sense, decolonisation is complete."[35]

The colonial system has denied the colonized's existence as a human being and now being independent, the native asks himself/herself the same question: Who am I after all? The disruption of colonialism has ruined the individuality and self-consciousness of the 'Negroes,'[36] and this state of the living dead must be surmounted as soon as possible to regain individual pride and honour. The colonial "vampire has

---

[33] Frantz Fanon, *Critical Perspectives*, ed. Anthony C. Alessandrini (London and New York: Routledge, 1999) 238.
[34] Ibid. 242.
[35] Raymond F. Betts, *Decolonisation* (London and New York: Routledge, 1998) 70.
[36] derogative term used for black people at the time of colonialism and beyond

transformed the natives into an animate corpse, one who breathes and walks, but whose life has 'ebbed away.'"[37] According to Ngugi wa Thiong'o,

> Imperialism introduced mass poverty and cross regional underdevelopment. Capitalism introduced plenty and possibilities of the conquest of hunger: capitalism ensured poverty and mass starvation on a scale unknown before. Capitalism and the development of science and technology introduced the possibilities of the conquest of nature: capitalism by its uncontrolled use and exploitation of natural resources ensured the virtual dominance of nature over man by way of droughts and desertification. Capitalism introduced a new medical science to conquer diseases: capitalism through its selective prescription of medical care, at least in the colonies, ensured a disease-ridden population who now lacked help from the herbalists and psychiatrists whose practises had been condemned as devilry.[38]

The loss of identity and customs means that the decolonised African has to redefine his identity, to create a new language or rather a language that fits the purpose of rising from the chaos of violence to a state of self-respect. The post-colonial text represents a means to fulfil this task because it is a blend of different styles and influences that mirrors African reality and distortion; thus, Africans and non-Africans, i.e. other colonised peoples, come to terms with a new identity. It has been the role of the writers after independence to reinterpret the world, to initiate the process of finding or rather constructing a new world. "To conceive an independent national identity, postcolonial writers concentrated on developing a symbolic vocabulary that was recognizably indigenous...and yet at the same time intelligible within a global grammar of post-war politics."[39] Thus, reviving the tradition of oral story telling and mythical stories meant restating a new self-definition. Stories of family and compound life were told, which not only presented "traditional ways but figured communal and national togetherness from within, using symbols of recognizably local derivation."[40] Moses Isegawa, for instance, depicts the traditional life of Uganda before, during and after independence in 1962, and defines the sense of alienation experienced by the colonized people. The writer tries to win the battle against the former master by telling his/her own stories and re-educating the reader. Africa had been a rich place with ancient traditions and customs, even richer than

---

[37] Fanon, *Critical Perspectives* 247.
[38] Ngugi wa Thiong'o, *Decolonising the Mind. The Politics of Language in African Literature* (London: James Currey, 1986) 66.
[39] Elleke Boehmer, *Colonial and Postcolonial Literature. Migrant Metaphors* (Oxford: Oxford UP, 1995) 187.
[40] Ibid. 187.

Europe; it was not the fringe, the 'other,' but a living presence ignored by the 'others.' The protagonists are not considered to be passive on-lookers anymore but active characters who fight for the survival of their own culture, plotting, making mistakes, failing or succeeding. The colonizer had denied the existing pre-European world but then the African writers began to place the natives into the historical context as active representatives and rulers of the world around them. This applies also to Chinua Achebe who "presents a view-from-within of his people's past. It is fitting therefore that *Things Fall Apart* assigns to the status of footnote the white man's presumptuous history mentioned at the end of the novel, the District Commissioner's 'Pacification of the Primitive Tribes of the Lower Niger.'"[41]

The new aim was not only to rewrite history in order to correct the distorted vision, but at the same time create symbols for a new national identity; it envisions the journey of a character like Mugezi into adulthood: the 'idyllic' childhood and dawn of self-consciousness, the loss of self-identity and roots, home motherland, beloved people, search of identity and problems in coming to terms with the wreckage of war and independence. Moreover, in search for a new identity, the protagonist returns to the colonial city and "gratifies his appetite for white women...by being her master."[42] Jean Veneuse goes one step further and states that his desire was "that white flesh that has been forbidden to us Negroes as long as white men have ruled the world, so that without my knowledge I am attempting to revenge myself on a European woman for everything that her ancestors have inflicted on mine throughout the centuries." (Veneuse quoted in Fanon: 1967, 70) In other words, they find access to the master of the white world through white women. This lack of self-assurance stems from early childhood experiences as a result of a "lack of love and understanding." (Guex quoted in Fanon: 1967, 73) Simply to be the 'other' is the starting point for self-reflection, which the decolonised hopes to regain through his relationship with the white woman. It is a kind of disruptive history, which calls for a redefinition of the symbols of life. Joseph Conrad and Chinua Achebe depicted the journey of the white man into the 'heart of darkness' whereas Isegawa sends his protagonist to Europe, from the hinterland to the city.

The 'new' transformed English language as a constituent of reality is used to write about the new identity because first, English has become a lingua franca for Nigeria and other countries, and therefore, stands for 'national unity.' Secondly, "English

---

[41] Ibid. 196.
[42] Fanon, *Black Skin, White Masks* 69.

was...so much a part of Nigerian life as to qualify as an African language."[43] English has developed into an international language which is formed into different englishes according to the various cultures. This multiplicity of forms of expression is called "boomeranging or switchback, where the once-colonized take the artefacts of the former master and make them their own."[44] By using proverbs, oral tradition and local idioms the writers form that 'alien' English into a language that has a spirit of its own. Salman Rushdie writes in his *Imaginary Homelands* in 1982 "...we can't simply use the language in the way the British did...it needs remaking for our own purposes."[45] As a matter of fact, elements of magic realism highlight the mythical and fantastic within the story and show the distorted displacement of the colonies. The multitude of the elements is in contrast to the motherland Europe with its restricted point of view. Elleke Boehmer confirms this by claiming,

> The postcolonial writer flamboyantly crosses, fragments and parodies different narrative styles and perspectives. Local contexts are reflected in the inclusion ...of untranslated words, obscure proverbs. The writer introduces a noise of voices that resists easy decoding. A similar effect is created where a work cites cultural information...which cannot be deciphered without background knowledge.[46]

Equipped with a language of its own, the ex-colonial writer is a cosmopolitan concentrating on retaining thematic and political connections with a national background. The colonized returns 'home' and writes from the metropolis expressing the disillusionment about the neo-colonial world. Boehmer calls it "dislocation," which helps the author to observe history from the distance and to expand "cultural and aesthetic experiences."[47] The aim of decolonisation is to put into question the superiority of the Western mentality and rationality, and to dismantle the centre. Postcolonial literature means exploring the past and recognizing the difference between comprehending and understanding: to understand indigenous literature means to know about it, and it demands serious work and the throwing off of ignorance and blindness, prejudices and stereotypes.

---

[43] Boehmer, *Colonial and Postcolonial Literature* 209.
[44] Ibid. 210.
[45] Salman Rushdie, *Imaginary Homelands: Essays and Criticism 1981-1991* (London: Granta, 1991) 17.
[46] Boehmer, *Colonial and Postcolonial Literature* 206.
[47] Ibid. 241.

III. Heart of Darkness
III.1. The Life and Works of Joseph Conrad

Originally named Jòsepf Teodor Konrad Korzeniowski, Conrad was born in 1857 to Polish parents in the Russian-dominated Ukraine. His parents, leading Polish patriots were found guilty of conspiring against the Russians and were exiled to the far-northern province of Vologda, their four-year-old son going with them. Partly as a result of this hardship, both parents died young, leaving Conrad orphaned at the age of eleven. His uncle, Thaddeus Bobrowski, took on the young Conrad, becoming his guardian and mentor. When he was sixteen, he left Poland for France to fulfil his early ambition to go to sea. Joining a ship in Marseille, Conrad spent four unsettled years, travelling mainly to and from the West Indies. It is during this time that he was allegedly involved in gunrunning, as well as running up huge gambling debts on borrowed money. He narrowly escaped death when he attempted suicide by shooting himself in the chest-the bullet missed his heart. In 1878 Conrad entered the British Merchant Navy, where he remained for the next sixteen years, rising to the position of Master Mariner. His time at sea, travelling widely to Singapore, Australia, the Belgian Congo (which later formed the basis of *Heart of Darkness*), Bombay and the West Indies, provided rich material for his stories. Becoming a naturalized Briton in 1886, Conrad finally settled for good in England in 1894 to devote himself to his writing. His first book, *Almeyer's Folly*, was published in 1895, the same year as his marriage to Jessie George. He followed this in 1896 with *An Outcast of the Islands*. Conrad's best writing is generally thought to be *The Nigger of 'Narcissus'* (1897), *Lord Jim* (1900), *Nostromo* (1904), *The Secret Agent* (1907) and *Victory* (1915). Although Conrad gained wide popularity after the publication of *Chance* in 1913, the quality of his later books deteriorated. This was due, at least in part, to the increasing ill health. Joseph Conrad died in 1924, leaving his last novel, *Suspense*, unfinished.

Heart of Darkness is based around Conrad's own disastrous experiences in the Congo in 1890.

In 1868, when he was a boy of nine, Conrad had been staring at a map of Africa. Pointing with his finger to the blank space that was the then unexplored heart of the continent, he said, "When I grow up I shall go there."[48] Twenty-one years later and in

---

[48] Joseph Conrad, *A Personal Record* (London: J.M. Dent & Sons, 1912) 13.

a different country, Conrad decided to make good on his boyhood promise. The blank space on the map of Africa was no longer blank; it was the Belgian Congo. Conrad decided to ask for the job of captain on one of the steamers that explored the centre of that territory.

Thus, in September of 1889, a letter was presented to Albert Thys, acting head of the Société Anonyme Belge pour les Commerce du Haut-Congo, recommending Captain Korzeniowski for the job. In January of 1890, Captain Korzeniowski (or Conrad, as he will be called from now on) wrote to an aunt by marriage, Madame Marguerite Poradowska, asking her to see what she could do to help him to obtain his appointment. Madame Poradowska was a woman of thirty, beautiful, and surrounded by a circle of influential friends. If anyone in Brussels could help Conrad, she could. On the fifth of February, Conrad began a trip from England to the Ukraine, where he was to visit relatives. He stopped off in Brussels to see Madame Poradowska, and then continued his trip. He spent several months in the Ukraine, but he corresponded with Madame Poradowska about his hoped-for job. Finally, on April 29, 1890, Conrad arrived for a second time in Brussels, this time to sign a contract to act as a riverboat pilot on the Congo River in Africa. On May 11, 1890, he set out for Bordeaux, France, where he would get a boat that would carry him off to Africa. The story Marlow tells in *Heart of Darkness*, about how he came to go to Africa, is almost exactly the same in the important details as the experience that Conrad had in 1889-1890. From the comparison of the diary that Conrad kept of his Congo adventures with the part of the story that takes place in Africa, it can be noticed how closely Conrad followed the details of his actual experience when he wrote his story. However, it was not until the last year of the nineteenth century that he wrote *Heart of Darkness* (not published until 1902), which can be seen in many ways as the first twentieth century novel.

III.2. Introduction to *Heart of Darkness*

Four friends are waiting on a cruising yawl for the turn of the tide in the sea-reach of the Thames. Marlow tells of his new job as a river-steamer captain for a Continental trading company. He goes out on a French ship to the mouth of the big Congo River. On reaching the Company's station he is horrified by what he describes as the slow death of the native workers. He begins to hear of a Mr Kurtz, a first-class agent and at the same time Marlow's aim. The next stage of Marlow's journey is a two-hundred-mile tramp with native carriers to the Central Station, where he finds that his steamer is sunk. While repairing the vessel, he gathers more information about Kurtz, who seems to become a symbol for Marlow's journey. When they finally reach the last station, they are greeted by arrows, which kill the helmsman. The white passengers fire futilely into the bush, but the steamer's whistle finally puts an end to the attack. While at the station Marlow realises that Kurtz is mentally ill as he participates in cannibalistic rites. Marlow rescues Kurtz from totally going mad and at the same time he is allowed to peep over the edge of reason. Kurtz dies on the steamer's return, after prolonged discourse about his past and plans. When the boy at the end announces that Kurtz is dead, Marlow realises the hollowness of life in general.

Heart of Darkness was in no way intended to provide an accurate description of Africa but it is a version of the continent as seen through late nineteenth-century European eyes.[49] Conrad had signed a contract with the Sociètè Anonyme Belge pour le Commerce du Haut-Congo, a commercial company Stanley had been associated with, then headed by the unsavoury M.A. Thys. The understanding was that Conrad was to command a river steamer for the duration of the three-year contract, but things went badly wrong. Conrad arrived in Kinshasa on August 2, but discovered that the ship he was to command was disabled. He was then assigned as second-in command to a captain L.R. Koch leading a relief expedition in the steamer *Roi des Belges* to Stanley Falls; the agent at the Stanley Falls station, Georges Antoine Klein, had become very ill. The ship arrived September 1, by which time Koch had also been taken ill. On the instructions of Camille Delcommune, Acting Manager of the

---

[49] the following passage is taken from *'Heart of Darkness': Joseph Conrad*, ed. D.C.R.A. Goonetilleke (London: Broadview Literary Books, 1995) 10.

Company, who was also among the party, Conrad was put in command of the ship for the return journey. As well as carrying the invalid Klein and Koch the steamer pulled two barges, probably filled with ivory. Klein died on board on September 21, shortly before the ship reached Kinshasa. Conrad was then to have accompanied Alexandre Delcommune on a new expedition on the Kasaii River to the Katanga region, which was to have lasted several months.

III.3. Congo Free State: Early History

Present-day Zaire, one of the largest nations in Africa, was known as the Belgian Congo from 1908 until 1960, when it gained its independence.[50] At Conrad's times it was called "L'Ètat Indépendent du Congo," the Congo Free State. But the Congo was Belgian from 1884 onwards, thanks to a conference called in Berlin in 1884 by Otto von Bismark. The Congo had been open to exploration and exploitation before, as Scot Dr. David Livingston had gone there in 1856, to be found by the Americanised Welshman Henry Morton Stanley in 1871. Livingston and Stanley, however, had been preceded by Portuguese, Dutch and French pioneers. The central event in the colonization of Africa was the Berlin Conference of 1884-85, at which the colonial powers carved up the continent among themselves. It became the Congo Free State in 1885, with King Leopold II of Belgium as its independent owner. In fact, until 1876, King Leopold II of Belgium had merely sat back and watched with interest. He organized a meeting in Brussels, the International Geographical Conference, to discuss a plan to open to civilization the unknown territory of the Congo. Leopold divided the country into sixteen districts, each governed by a commissioner who rendered the local chiefs impotent. Some of these officials went on to build personal fortunes by collecting taxes from the natives, and since few of the natives had anything to give but their labour, the commissioners were slaveholders, and the Congolese were slaves. Leopold, in turn, received a portion of all profits made by his administrators, so it was in his interest to make sure that when Africans rebelled

---

[50] the following information about the historical situation of the Congo is taken from Maurice N. Hennessy, "The Congo Free State: A Brief History, 1876 to 1908," *Congo* (London: Pall Mall Press, 1961) 13-27.

against the sentries who guarded them while they worked out their taxes, they be taught a swift and brutal lesson. The Congo was far from Europe, and Leopold succeeded in convincing the Europeans and Belgians that violence was only used in extreme cases and that those natives were prone to turn on their own people because they were naturally considered to be barbarians and cannibals.

Ivory, the most valuable commodity, had become a Belgian monopoly. Non-Belgian traders caught carrying it could be summarily shot, either by Leopold's army-trained representatives or by their sentries. The spirit of bitterness and hatred generated in the people was quite terrifying, but little could be done about it as there was not enough control in the area to prevent the various agents from misusing their power. Leopold retained control of the Congo Free State until his death in 1908. Leopold ruled absolutely in the Congo, so absolutely that he was able to bequeath his so-called Independent State of Belgium in 1895. At the time of his death in 1908, the Free State became the Belgian Congo and remained under Belgian domination until 1960, when the demand for independence could no longer be denied.

III.4. Conrad's Personal Experience in the Congo

Joseph Conrad wrote in his diary, "Going up that river was like travelling back to the earliest beginnings of the world, when vegetation rioted on the earth and the big trees were kings."[51] But we soon realise that he was also scared of the African continent when Conrad wrote to his aunt on May 15, 1890, "In the meantime I am comparatively happy, which is all one can hope for in this wicked world."[52] She then in return claimed, "He left Europe full of energy and thrilling expectations, with ideas about a civilizing mission"[53] but "He returned gravely ill, never to regain fully his good health, disillusioned, memories to be used later in his famous story 'Heart of

---

[51] Joseph Conrad, "The Congo Diary," *Tales of Hearsay and Last Essays* (London: J.M. Dent & Sons, 1955) 7.

[52] *The Collected Letters of Joseph Conrad, Volume 1, 1861-1897*, eds. Frederick R. Karl and Laurence Davies (Cambridge: Cambridge UP, 1983) 51.

[53] Tadeusz Bobrowski to Conrad, 24 June 1890, *Conrad's Polish Background*, ed. Zdzislaw Najder (Oxford: Oxford UP,1964) 129.

Darkness'..."[54] Apparently he had not been able to cope with the darkness as Marlow asks himself "could we handle that dumb thing, or would it handle us?...Yet somehow it didn't bring any image with it-no more if I had been told an angel or a fiend was in there."[55]

Reading through his Congo diary, the reader is immediately struck by the description of his journey. After all, it was not pleasant for him because he repetitively complains about mosquitoes, people speaking ill of each other, frogs and other animals. He mentioned the encounter with a dead man who had apparently been shot, three women with red eyes and red hair, features that seemed ugly and beastly to him.[56] Conrad regretted bitterly to have gone to the Congo when he wrote to his aunt, "Everything is repellent to me. Men and things, but men above all."[57] As a matter of fact, this speaks volumes about the characterization of all the Europeans, except Kurtz, and we now understand his hatred and contempt towards imperialistic exploitation:

> It is a story of the Congo. There is no love interest in it and no woman – only incidentally. The exact locality is not mentioned. All the bitterness of those days, all my puzzled wonder as to the meaning of all I saw – all my indignation at masquerading philanthropy – have been with me again, while I wrote. The story is simple – there is hardly any description. The most common incidents are related- the life in a lonely station on the Kassai. I have divested myself of everything but pity – and some scorn – while putting down the insignificant events that bring on the catastrophe. Upon my word I think it is a good story – and not so gloomy – not fanciful – alas! I think it is interesting – some may find it a bore![58]

It should be clear that the story is more concentrated on "the criminality of inefficiency and pure selfishness when tackling the civilizing work in Africa…It is less concentrated upon individuals."[59]

Nevertheless, he is very clear in stating "What I distinctly admit is the fault of having made Kurtz too symbolic or rather symbolic at all. But the story being mainly a vehicle for conveying a batch of personal impressions I gave the rein to my mental

---

[54] *Congo Diary and Other Uncollected Pieces*, ed. Zdzislaw Najder (New York: Doubleday, 1978) 1.
[55] Joseph Conrad, *Heart of Darkness* (London: Penguin Books, 1902) 38. Further references to the book will be made with parenthetical documentation.
[56] Ibid. 7-16.
[57] *The Collected Letters of Joseph Conrad*, 61-63.
[58] Ibid. 293-94.
[59] *The Collected Letters of Joseph Conrad Volume II*, 139-140.

laziness and took the line of the least resistance. This is then the whole Apologia pro Vita Kurtzii – or rather for the tardiness of his vitality."[60] Although he admitted having exaggerated the symbolism in *Heart of Darkness*, his achievement was to make people feel, hear, and at the same time see what was happening in a remote country which was feared by many to be still a harbour of savagery, but the majority did not realise that Africa in general was "also that glimpse of truth for which you have forgotten to ask."[61] Once again, we are given clear evidence of real life occurrences that must have influenced Conrad in writing *Heart of Darkness*:

> The two events that did most to bring Leopold's Congo under public scrutiny after Conrad's time were the 1891-94 war between Leopold's forces and the Arab slave-traders and the murder of Charles Stokes, English citizen and renegade missionary, by Belgian officials in 1895...Arabs were sent to punish the natives; many women and children were taken, and twenty-one heads were brought to Stanley Falls, and have been used by Captain Rom as a decoration round a flower-bed in front of his house.[62]

Charles Stokes, an Irish ex-missionary turned trader, was executed in the Eastern Congo in 1895 by order of Lothair, on the pretext that he was supplying guns to a powerful Afro-Arab slaver. There was a public outcry when news of execution reached England. "Stocke's fate is seen as the possible destiny of the harlequin, the young Russian adventurer whose presence as a freelance trader is savagely resented by the manager."[63] Conrad wanted to highlight his encounter with the ruthlessness of white colonialism, which pushed the African continent into a pitch-black pit:

> Conrad's stress on cannibalism, his identification of African customs with violence, lust, and madness, his metaphors of bestiality, death, and darkness, his suggestion that travelling in Africa is like travelling backward in time to primeval, infantile, but also hellish stages of existence – these features of the story are drawn from the repertoire of Victorian imperialism and racism that painted an entire continent dark.[64]

---

[60] Ibid. 460-1.
[61] Joseph Conrad, "The Preface (1897)," *The Nigger of the Narcissus* (New York: Norton, 1979) 145-48.
[62] E.J. Glave, "Cruelty in the Congo Free State." *Century Magazine* 54 (1897): 706.
[63] M.M. Mahood, *The Colonial Encounter: A Reading of Six Novels* (London: Rex Collings, 1977) 10.
[64] Patrick Brantlinger, "*Heart of Darkness*: Anti-Imperialism, Racism, or Impressionism?" *Case Studies in Contemporary Criticism. 'Heart of Darkness': Joseph Conrad*, ed. Ross C. Murfin, 2nd ed. (Boston: Bedford, 1996) 285.

III.5. Conrad as a Child of the 19th Century
III.5.1. "Racism" and Reactions

The end of the 19th century was the high time of imperialism and racism. The Victorians would not think of non-whites in terms of words other than 'nigger' or 'savage;' they were thinking in terms of white and black, superiority and inferiority, 'we' and the 'other,' Europeans and Africans, civilized and savage, light and darkness. It is true that Conrad's depiction of his natives in *Heart of Darkness* can be interpreted as racist by modern criticism because of the repeated use of the word 'nigger' and the description of black people as savage, dark and brutal cannibals who practise 'unspeakable rites' in order to satiate their lust and hunger. Accordingly, Chinua Achebe accuses Conrad of being ..."a bloody racist..." and he throws in the question "...whether a novel which celebrates this dehumanisation, which depersonalises a portion of the human race, can be called a great work of art. My answer is: No, it cannot."[65] It will not be discussed whether *Heart of Darkness* is a great work of art or not, but the important fact is that Conrad described the treatment of the people in the Congo by the European imperialists and colonizers, especially the Belgians. As it has already been mentioned, it is true that he portrays the Africans in a derogative way when he describes the helmsman at the point of death for instance, but his book strongly reflects the attitude of his time towards Africa, and he particularly condemns the European harbingers of light. It is a tale about the hollowness of the European enterprise and their barbaric behaviour towards others they do not understand because they have been alienated from their own heritage and origin to a great extent. Murfin defines Kurtz's post-scriptum as "the appalling revelation of the naked racist brutality at the heart of Kurtz and the heart of imperialism: 'Exterminate all the Brutes!'"[66] As far as extermination is concerned, the brutes are not the African or Congolese natives, but the white man with his mission. After having observed the mysteries of life, after having been caressed by the wilderness for intruding, after having been punished for exploiting the natives and nature by stealing ivory, Kurtz realised the rottenness of imperialism and the white man; that is when he wants to exterminate all the brutes, but the white brutes. Light is

---

[65] Chinua Achebe, "An Image of Africa," *The Massachusetts Review* 18 (1977) 788.
[66] '*Heart of Darkness*': *Joseph Conrad* 18.

dire, too clean and therefore, a lie; Brussels, his aunt, the two women at the company in Brussels, the doctor, are all a modern lie. On the contrary, the black wilderness is new, fascinating, unique and not a sham. It can appear to be menacing, brutal and even violent, but after all, it is something innocent and genuine.

A remarkable fact is that Marlow condemns Belgian imperialism but "his intention is to exclude the English from criticism" because "Conrad felt a moral obligation to the English, …he believed that true liberty was possible only under the English flag. Finally, his story was intended to appear as a serial in the conservative *Blackwood's Magazine*."[67] Felix Mnthali argues, "Conrad attacks Europe's scramble for Africa…This attack is all the same neutralised by Conrad's acceptance of one of the cornerstones of modern imperialism, namely, racism." (quoted in Goonetilleke: 1990: 85) On the one hand Conrad is fascinated by English imperialism, and on the other disgusted and horrified by the Belgian mission in the Congo. True, the Belgian exploitation of the Congo was imperialistic brutality at its peak, but also England was more than just a cog in the machine. "The element of weakness in Conrad's presentation of African realities can be related to his attitude towards and knowledge of them. He has certain conventional attitudes towards Negroes and knew little about them."[68] The same can be applied to British imperialism. My theory is that those who lack a national identity tend to be more racist than others because they have difficulty in coming to terms with their own origins. Conrad's family had been exiled to Russia, his parents died very young and he left the country relatively early to go to France; consequently, he did not believe in his identity because he had been stripped of his origins.

> The two minds in which Conrad found himself about civilization were the Polish mind which saw it as a mere conquest and rapine masquerading in the guise of philanthropy, and the English mind clinging to the faith that some work of real benefit could be done. In *Heart of Darkness* the English mind speaks through Marlow, who withholds the truth from the Intended because he realizes that we are sustained by our fidelities.[69]

---

[67] Gary Adelmann, *'Heart of Darkness': Search for the Unconscious* (Boston: Twayne Publishers, 1987) 47, 61.
[68] D.C.R.A. Goonetilleke, *Joseph Conrad: Beyond Culture and Background* (London: Macmillan, 1990) 87-8.
[69] Mahood, *The Colonial Encounter* 34.

Conrad had difficulty in facing colonialism because he wrote things like "every nation's conquests are paved with good intentions"[70] and then that "the criminality of inefficiency and pure selfishness when tackling the civilizing work in Africa is a justifiable idea."[71] Conrad was a child nurtured by his century because he was highly influenced by contemporaries such as Eduard von Hartmann, who believed that the Africans "were an inferior and doomed people."[72] It bears resemblance to Jonathan Swift's satirical pamphlet and it is not surprising that "'Exterminate all the brutes' is Conrad's modest proposal."[73]

Conrad wrote, "I know that a novelist lives in his work. He stands there, the only reality in an invented world, amongst imaginary things, happenings and people. Writing about them, he is only writing about himself. Every novel contains an element of autobiography – and this can hardly be denied, since the creator can only explain himself in his creations."[74]

III.6. The Narrator and Conrad's Narrative Technique

Heart of Darkness is written as a narrative within a narrative. The first narrator never enters into the story itself; he merely describes events that occur on the deck of a yacht, the Nellie, anchored in the Thames in the middle of London. The first narrator describes the deck of the Nellie where he and a group of four other persons have gathered: the Director of Companies, the Lawyer, the Accountant, and Marlow, "'the only man of us who still 'followed the sea.'" (Conrad 7) It is Marlow who narrates the adventures in the Congo. From time to time, the scene moves back to the deck of the yacht, and the first narrator picks up the story. Why has Conrad gone to the trouble of introducing a character, Marlow between the story to be told and the

---

[70] Avrom Fleischman, *Conrad's Politics: Community and Anarchy in the Fiction of Joseph Conrad* (Baltimore: Johns Hopkins, 1967) 106.
[71] Jocelyn Baines, *Joseph Conrad: A Critical Biography* (London: Weidenfeld & Nicholson, 1960) 120.
[72] John E. Saveson, "Conrad's View of Primitive Peoples in *Lord Jim* and *Heart of Darkness*," *Modern Fiction Studies* 16 (1970) 174-5.
[73] Frances B. Singh, "The Colonialistic Bias of *Heart of Darkness*," *Conradiana* 10 (1978) 50.
[74] Arthur Simmons, *Notes on Joseph Conrad: With some Unpublished Letters* (London: Arthur Simmons and Meyers & Co., 1925) 15-18.

author, Conrad himself? One possibility is that Conrad felt he needed an additional character, not identified with the 'pilgrims' of the trading company, or with the author himself. The function of this character would be to establish a norm against which we can compare the actions of the other characters. Marlow stands for man as he usually is, while the 'pilgrims' and Kurtz stand for men deviated from the norm. If this is the case, however - if both Conrad and Marlow are represented in the story - we must be careful about ascribing feelings and ideas of Marlow to Conrad. Although we can expect Conrad to agree with most of Marlow's opinions, Conrad is not Marlow; the two are separate.

"The anonymous frame narrator is a beneficiary of imperialism, yet, like Marlow before his river journey, he is ignorant of imperial realities. He undergoes a process of education as he listens to Marlow's tale… Marlow is essentially a projection of the middleclass Englishman, still rather extravert and enthusiastic about British imperialism."[75] Marlow is compared to a Buddha who relates his tale; moreover, he is a seeker of truth and experiences the darkness through his journey to the darkness of 'white humanity.' Marlow prefers the nightmare of Kurtz to the nightmare of the pilgrims and the other colonial employees. Those are hollow, but Kurtz inspires people because he discovers the truth behind appearance; he sees the absolute nullity of his former life and of the colonial enterprise.

Conrad's invention of Marlow as narrator gave him the dual advantage of first-person intimacy and anonymity. Lying is at the heart of the story, not because he does not want to share the revelation, but too many people would not comprehend the truth. "The use of a first-person narrative, through the agency of Marlow, was necessary so that Conrad could gain aesthetic distance, and the reader could identify with an average man thrown into an abnormal situation."[76] The mirror effect is visible in the "most realistic passages in *Heart of Darkness*, Marlow's rhetorical addresses to the audience. In these moments Marlow defines himself - and is defined by the frame narrator/listener – as a figure outside fiction whose function is to probe and emphasise the actuality of his act of telling."[77] The frame narrator has a double function: describing the setting and introducing the characters on the vessel. Another

---

[75] *'Heart of Darkness': Joseph Conrad* 30-1.

[76] Frederick R. Karl, "Introduction to the *Danse Macabre*: Conrad's *Heart of Darkness*," *'Heart of Darkness': Joseph Conrad, A Case Study in Contemporary Criticism*, ed. Ross C. Murfin (New York: St. Martin's Press, 1989) 134.

[77] Richard Ambrosini, *Conrad's Fiction as Critical Discourse* (Cambridge: Cambridge UP, 1991) 85.

important function is his recollection of the Roman conquest of Great Britain when he compares the Thames to the Congo River, "What greatness had not floated on the ebb of that river into the mystery of an unknown earth!...The dreams of men, the seed of commonwealths, the germs of empires." (Conrad 7) "There is the bird's eye view, simulated and stimulated through the relativistic treatment of space and time that parallels the Congo with the Thames, the African depths with pre-Roman Britain; and, above all, a distancing split of the narrative voice."[78] European colonial conquest can be compared to that of the Romans:

> to the Romans, the people of Britain were barbarians; now when the Europeans come to Africa, the Africans in comparison seem savage, but deep down in the European breast there still lurks the old savagery... When the Romans looked down upon the people of Britain, and the Europeans upon natives, it was because they felt they had achieved a much higher civilization than the people they were confronting and conquering.[79]

As a matter of fact, *Heart of Darkness* is very symbolical although Conrad himself admitted that perhaps he made it too symbolical at all. Nevertheless, when we imagine the journey up the River Congo to the Inner Station, the attack of the natives, Kurtz's hut surrounded by the poles with human heads, the native mistress crying as they take Kurtz away, and many other scenes, the first impression is the pictorial character of the book or rather the journey. It is like a dream, which cannot be explained or pinned down on the one hand, and a huge tapestry on the other. The search for Conrad reminds me of Dante's *Divine Comedy* with his descent into hell and the journey up to heaven through the purgatory, but also of Botticelli's drawings of the *Divine Comedy*. The tale he narrates is one he cannot suppress; that is why it has been compared to Coleridge's *The Rime of the Ancient Mariner*, to *Everyman* and Bunyan's *Pilgrim's Progress*. I would compare *Heart of Darkness* to Forster's *A Passage to India* (the Marabar Caves) and Arnundhati's *The God of Small Things* because both works try to draw the attention to the mystery of life itself. Cedric Watts compares *Heart of Darkness* to Faust, Charlotte Bronte's *Wuthering Heights*, Chaucer's *Canterbury Tales*, Coleridge's *The Ancient Mariner*, and Dante's *Divine Comedy*. "Like Dante...Marlow can summon up a measure of sympathy for those

---

[78] Joseph Dobrinsky, *The Artist in Conrad's Fiction: A Psychocritical Study* (London: UMI, 1989) 19.
[79] C.P. Sarvan, "Racism and the *Heart of Darkness*," *The International Fiction Review* 7 (1980) 8.

who succumb to their emotions or appetites and reserve unmeasured scorn for those who pervert reason."[80]

Marlow descends into the 'apparent' heart of darkness to rescue Kurtz, the emissary of light, and finds out about the truth. "Marlow's European conception of blackness as inferior or evil is undermined when he finds no moral darkness in the black inhabitants of Africa, but is forced to link many of the traditional negative connotations of darkness with the colour white."[81] Marlow recognizes darkness as the primary element of life and attributes to the light qualities such as violence, corruption, death, blindness, and ignorance. The reference to the Buddha-like stature of Marlow at the end of the story tells us, "Marlow's narrative is essentially a self-examining meditation."[82] For Marlow the meaning of an episode was not inside like a kernel but outside. That is, for him the meaning should not be looked for in the message but in the way in which the story is told. "The man in the name whom the young Marlow had once been unable to envision has now become for the old Marlow the ghost in the mind whom it is impossible to exorcise. In the end the man in the name survives as a man in Marlow; he has been transformed into an integral part of Marlow himself, just as he has in all of us who have heard his voice and seen his image."[83]

Conrad's writing technique is called delayed decoding, and a perfect example would be the attack of the natives with the arrows in which Marlow at first is not aware of the fact that he is attacked, but refers to the arrows as little wooden sticks; moments later he realises the danger of the situation and the actual arrows speeding by. (Conrad, 64) This technique is quite gripping

> since it combines the forward temporal progression of the mind, as it receives messages from the outside world, with the much slower reflexive process of making out their meaning...Conrad presented the protagonist's immediate sensations, and thus made the reader aware of the gap between impression and understanding; the delay in bridging the gap enacts the disjunction between the event and the observer's trailing understanding of it.[84]

---

[80] William M. Hagen, "*Heart of Darkness* and the Process of Apocalypse Now," Conradiana 13 (1981) 46.

[81] Cedric Watt, "*Heart of Darkness*," *The Cambridge Companion to Joseph Conrad*, ed. J.H. Stape (Cambridge: Cambridge UP, 1996) 189.

[82] Ibid. 193.

[83] Peter Edgerly Firchow, *Envisioning Africa: Racism and Imperialism in Conrad's 'Heart of Darkness'* (Kentucky: Kentucky UP, 2000) 80.

[84] Ian Watt, "Impressionism and Symbolism in *Heart of Darkness*," *Conrad in the Nineteenth Century* (Berkeley and Los Angeles: California UP, 1979) 174.

The method has also the advantage of convincing the reader of the reality of the experience described by the narrator. The readers are bombarded by multiple impressions and they are requested to find the meaning and at the same time to interpret it. "By holding back information and moving forward and backward in time, Conrad catches up and involves the reader in a moral situation, makes the reader's emotions follow a course analogous to that of the characters."[85]

III.7. The Notion of Work/Language Within the Dream-like Journey

The notion of work is very important throughout the book because it prevents Marlow from taking one step further and penetrating into the light. "A man is a worker. If he is not that he is nothing. Just nothing – like a mere adventurer."[86] Marlow would have experienced the same revelation as Kurtz if he had not had to concentrate on his boat and the expedition in general. "The duality of Marlow's character mirrors an old-age conflict between order, discipline, restraint – without which civilization would quickly perish – and a more primeval impulse to yield to repressed instincts." Work "... serves as a break against the accelerating descent into the self, it becomes nothing less than the central method of self-therapy in Conrad's universe."[87] Work prevents Marlow from following Kurtz and therefore, dying; Marlow catches a glimpse of the truth and is permitted to leave the darkness with a speck of light within his heart. He then decides to hold back what he has seen because humanity is destined to live on the surface and to be distracted by work so that its illusion may live on. "Marlow's short-lived rage parallels though on a smaller scale Kurtz's 'Exterminate all the Brutes'..."[88] He decides to live with the illusion of the surface truths, and simultaneously, he betrays Kurtz's demand for justice. The price for his lie at the end is that his suffering has just started; furthermore, he is forced to tell the tale again and again to convince people of its authenticity, but the question

---

[85] Thomas Moser, *Joseph Conrad: Achievement and Decline* (Cambridge: Harvard UP, 1957) 42.
[86] Joseph Conrad, "Well Done," *Notes on Life and Letters* (London: J.M. Dent & Sons, 1921) 189-91.
[87] Jeffrey Berman, *Joseph Conrad: Writing as Rescue* (New York: Astra Books, 1977) 55, 60.
[88] Ibid. 66.

remains whether the people to whom the story is told will believe it and recognise its core.

"Marlow commits himself to the yet unseen agent partly because Kurtz 'had come out equipped with moral ideas of some sort'. Anything would seem preferable to the demoralized greed and total cynicism of the others."[89] The white man was protected by work and society with its laws and watchful neighbours; actually those neighbours cared a lot about Victorian ethics and morals. When the wall crumbles, he has to face the light with his inborn energy. The hollow man will surrender to the darkness and see the truth, but it is a matter of restraint; Kurtz did not have such a restraint, at least not at the beginning, because he was hollow at the core. The heart of darkness is not dark in itself, but it lies in the darkness and has to be discovered in order to see, hear and feel the light within it. Once you see it, you will experience the horror because turning away from the truth again and becoming aware of the corruption and darkness of the westernised modern world, is a source of pain. Kurtz himself was a symbol, a voice, the personified darkness, the darkness which surrounded Marlow. "Is Kurtz the symbol of Marlow's own 'heart of darkness' - an embodiment of the destructive instinct of the European psyche that has made a voyeur, if not altogether a colonizer, of Marlow, and that has made a great slave plantation of Africa?"[90] Kurtz is the symbol of the destructive imperialistic forces that enslaved the black continent, but at the same time the figure of Kurtz presages the complete reversal of the symbolic meaning of 'heart of darkness.' That is to say that the Europeans themselves stand for destruction and blackness, and not the native Africans, who are depicted like savages. The white man, namely Kurtz, penetrates into Africa, discovers his kinship with the natives, but then realises that it is himself who is dark in his own heart; he is set loose from European restraint, and armed to the teeth, he tries to take advantage of the 'other.' Ivory is the mighty symbol and represents Europe and its hunger for power; Kurtz came to the Congo to civilize the savage customs of the natives. He had a noble zeal to perform, but then he realised that he embodied the crude and antagonistic forces of the real 'savage' people, namely the Europeans. It was then that he became one of them because he saw the horror behind the European façade. Moreover, he saw the people in Africa and sensed their nativity and sincerity but went mad when he visualised the corruption of the Europeans and modern society. "Kurtz's cry might

---

[89] Albert J. Guerard, "The Journey Within," *Conrad the Novelist* (Harvard: The President and the Fellows of Harvard College, 1958) 50.
[90] Adelmann, *Heart of Darkness* 9.

be a shriek of despair that after having accomplished so little he must now perish."[91] Black and white are two very important images in the story: Romans, women and their fate, Kurtz's painting of the woman with the torch vs. the white sepulchre. The same applies to Marlow, who is different from the others in that he is spiritually connected to Kurtz and his vision. He prefers the truth to the lies of civilization and therefore, despises the surface existence of the other colonizers. Once expelled to the barbaric traits in oneself, one either keeps up the façade or surrenders to the primordial instincts, which constitute the basis of the human being. Kurtz had the choice between the white Europe and the mysterious Africa and he decided to live rather than vegetate. Marlow, on the other hand, decides to lie to Kurtz's Intended because he believes that for her and many others it is of vital importance to carry on living with the lie of society.

Marlow despises the 'pilgrims' who fire into the bushes and condemns their imperialistic behaviour because it is them who are savage, not the blacks whose cannibalism seems to be accepted by Marlow as a part of the African way of life. "Marlow is so far from attributing any positive qualities to the whites that he coolly considers the possibility that it is disgust which keeps the cannibals from eating their employers and rejects it only because he realises that disgust is not a sufficient barrier for starving men."[92] After all, it is an intrusion on behalf of the white man who destroys the harmony of the black continent; obviously, they should stay away from the 'others.' Conrad describes his experience as "...the distasteful knowledge of the vilest scramble for loot that ever disfigured the history of human conscience and geographical exploration. What an end to the idealized realities of a boy's daydreams!"[93]

> Kurtz's degradation is...perhaps god-like; it is the effect of his setting himself apart from the earth – apart, even, from the language of the earth with which he had such magnificent facility... The primary reality is the suggested essence of the wilderness, the darkness that must remain hidden if a man is to survive morally; the second reality is a figurative reality like work...this reality of the second sort is simply a deluding activity, a fictitious play over the surface of things.[94]

---

[91] Karl, *'Heart of Darkness': Joseph Conrad, A Case Study in Contemporary Criticism* 130.
[92] *'Heart of Darkness': Joseph Conrad* 22.
[93] Joseph Conrad, "Geography and Some Explorers," *Tales of Hearsay and Last Essays*, ed. Richard Curle (London: J.M. Dent, 1926) 17.
[94] James Guetti, "The Failure of the Imagination," 1965, *Conrad: 'Heart of Darkness,' 'Nostromo' and 'Under Western Eyes,' A Casebook*, ed. C.B. Cox (London: Macmillan, 1981) 68,70.

Is death not a realisation of the futility, wraith of one's life? I think that is the reason why Kurtz was horrified by his vision. Is Marlow able to catch a glimpse of the truth beyond the surface? According to my interpretation of the story, he is aware of the realities which surround him; he is aware of them but cannot or rather does not want to accept them because all the meanings and experiences around him are unreal. Marlow lives a kind of dream and he explicitly tells his readers or listeners when he asks them "Do you see the story? Do you see anything? It seems to me I am trying to tell you a dream...it is impossible to convey the life-sensation of any given epoch of one's existence...We live, as we dream – alone." (Conrad 39) We are confronted with this dream sensation of the whole journey, and Marlow tells us about his conception of that dream. If he had not had all the work to do on board of the steamer, he would probably have been the next 'victim' or rather the next receiver through whom nature would have expressed itself. But as Marlow says, we live as we dream – alone; that is the outstanding thing about dreams in general. Many people have a different notion of their experiences and encounters, and it is open to interpretation. Through these interpretations they have the chance to filter out something special and unique. That is why Marlow tells his story to his fellow seamen on board of the vessel. The manager, the pilgrims and the natives on the steamer do not realise the presence of a greater and mightier force than they can ever produce because they live on the surface of reality with their language of society. Therefore, reality is beyond language; "Marlow himself embodies his experience. His physical presence both compensates for the limitations of language and helps explain them. He is literally and objectively the meaning of his own narrative. Only by seeing Marlow can his auditors ever hope to understand what he has been trying to tell them, and their ultimate failure is another triumph of the darkness."[95] Many critics complain about Conrad's depiction of the native protagonists as far as speech is concerned. Chinua Achebe claims that in depicting them as speechless, Conrad manifests his racist attitudes. As a matter of fact, language is something that operates mostly on the surface and consequently, not always grasps truth. The white man is equipped with language and tries to explain his futile existence whereas the natives do not have to speak because they do not live on the surface, which includes the condemnation of the 'other.' "One way to define the darkness is to say that it is incompatible with

---

[95] Jerry Wassermann, "Narrative Presence: The Illusion of Language in *Heart of Darkness*," *Critical Essays on Joseph Conrad* (Boston: G.K. Hall & Co, 1987) 102.

language."[96] The episode of the whistle on the steamer illustrates that the natives are afraid of the noise and are not to be influenced by futile talking. Another example is Marlow and the Intended who both speak the same language but talk in parallel universes. After all, there is the silence of the wilderness that expresses more than all the languages of the world. "Language is the psychic dress of civilized man...To reject language as a façade or a fiction is to open oneself to the possibility of understanding the true mysteries of the heart of darkness. But it is also to invite a kind of madness."[97] For Marlow Kurtz is the ultimate representative of society because he can change people with his speech, he is pure eloquence, he is a 'disembodied voice.' This voice survived the communion with the wilderness, which showed him his vain attempt to bring light to the darkness. It took revenge on him by letting him escape before dying and at the same time realise the vanity of the world Westerners were living in. Kurtz had dared to call out "My Intended, my ivory, my station, my river, my-everything belonged to him. It made me hold my breath in expectation of hearing the wilderness burst into a prodigious peal of laughter that would shake the fixed stars in their places." (Conrad 70) Nobody could understand that because all the others, except Marlow, lived in a society protected by laws, neighbours and policemen. The secret of surviving is to "breathe dead hippo, so to speak, and not be contaminated...All Europe contributed to the making of Kurtz." (Conrad 71) The International Society for the Suppression of Savage Customs expected him to fulfil his mission by offering the natives a piece of civilization. Contrarily, the natives and nature in general offered him something he could not resist, which was the ultimate truth behind the wall of ignorance. "He had the power to charm or frighten rudimentary souls into an aggravated witch-dance in his honour...it was a kind of partnership. He steered for me – I had to look after him, I worried about his deficiencies, and thus a subtle bond had been created, of which I only became aware when it was suddenly broken." (Conrad 73) To survive in the world means not to succumb to the truth, but to hide it; the work of civilization is basically an illusion, but since the alternative can spoil one's existence it must go on.

> It is work, then, that constructs the lie of civilization that hides humanity, necessarily, from the prehistoric truth about itself...Work does indeed restrain. Perhaps, however, the reason why people with hands busy about the work of the earth are restrained from seeing a

---

[96] J. Hillis Miller, *Poets of Reality: Six Twentieth Century Writers* (Cambridge: Harvard University Press, 1966) 36.
[97] Wassermann, *Critical Essays on Joseph Conrad* 105.

glimpse of the truth is not because they repress an unconscious world of the imagination that contains an ahistorical truth about the reality of forms, but because they are given no time to become conscious of the history of how the time of their lives had been wasted.[98]

Nevertheless, "Going up that river was like travelling back to the earliest beginnings of the world, when vegetation rioted on the earth and the big trees were kings" and with the help of work "...the reality fades. The inner truth is hidden – luckily, luckily." (Conrad 48-9) The steamer expedition was on its way into the past reality "...because we were travelling in the night of first ages, of those ages that are gone, leaving hardly a sign – and no memories." (Conrad 51)

III.8. Marlow's Discovery: A Choice of Nightmares

What did Kurtz see and what did Marlow discover? The second part of the question is the more challenging one because as I have already observed, Kurtz's glimpse penetrated into the unseen and unheard. He saw the essence of things and human nature; as a result, he suffered for the ultimate brutality of his fellow colonizers towards 'his people.' Darkness can be compared to mystery and innocence whereas whiteness is similar to corruption and destruction. Kurtz is a voice, which attracts and fascinates Marlow, and he has to speak to Kurtz in order to understand the ultimate silence. The wilderness took revenge on Kurtz for his invasion. Furthermore, in facing the abominable essence of the outside world, he turned away from the horror and dedicated his energy to the natives and their pure lives. Marlow comprehended the message the wilderness had spread out through Kurtz and "I remained to dream the nightmare out to the end, and to show my loyalty to Kurtz once more." (Conrad 100) Therefore, he had to choose between two nightmares: to bring the torch of light to Europe and spread the truth, or to erase Kurtz's outburst of sincerity and lie to the Intended. He chose the latter because he knew that the truth would destroy the surface of people's lives as the Congo, its river, and its inhabitants

---

[98] Thomas Brook, "Preserving and Keeping Order by Killing Time in *Heart of Darkness*," *Case Studies in Contemporary Criticism. Joseph Conrad: 'Heart of Darkness,'* ed. Ross C. Murfin, 2nd ed. (Boston: Bedford, 1996) 255.

were a "flabby, pretending, weak-eyed devil of a rapacious and pitiless folly." (Conrad 23) In a way, he remains loyal to Kurtz when he says, "…it was written I should be loyal to the nightmare of my choice." (Conrad 92) The horror speaks through Marlow when he sees the futility of the people back in Brussels who "dream their insignificant and silly dreams." (Conrad 102) He seems disgusted by the whiteness of the inhabitants of the 'other world' but he does not dare to tell them about Kurtz and the real light. He prefers them to keep up their illusion knowing that the truth would be devastating.

Kurtz's native woman embodies the spirit of the wilderness in the Congo while his Intended is the symbol of the western world, "she has chosen for herself a graveyard, where she can exist in comfort only through a lie…In contrast, the savage lives out her sexual urges as naturally as if she were a wild beast."[99] There is this choice of nightmares between the Intended and the savage woman; it is quite clear that the Intended lives a nightmare. On the contrary, the savage woman represents another nightmare because the Europeans are alienated from their inner-self and their past. They live the lie and condemn others who do not have the language to define the surface. Lionel Trilling gives us an interesting description of the situation by declaring,

> Whichever it is, to Marlow the fact that Kurtz could utter this cry at the point of death, while Marlow himself, when death threatens him, can know it only as a weary greyness, marks the difference between the ordinary man and a hero of the spirit. Is this not the essence of the modern belief about the nature of the artist, the man who goes down into that hell which is the historical beginning of the human soul, a beginning not outgrown but established in humanity as we know it now, preferring the reality of this heel to the bland lies of the civilization that has overlaid it?[100]

At the end Marlow is confronted with the Intended as a representative of the sterile life in Brussels and Europe. The Intended puts out her arms and her gesture reminds us of Kurtz's mistress when the expedition carried Kurtz away. "She is metamorphosed into the savage, for she too is a tragic figure, the prey of an incomprehensible passion."[101] "The Intended is Kurtz's heritage, his idea, the source of the momentum energizing his mistaken mission; in short, his intention."[102] The

---

[99] C.B. Cox, *Joseph Conrad: The Modern Imagination* (London: J.M. Dent & Sons, 1974) 46.
[100] Lionel Trilling, *Beyond Culture* (London: Secker and Warburg, 1966) 20-1.
[101] Cox, *Joseph Conrad: The Modern Imagination* 59.
[102] Robert Baker, "Watt's Conrad," *Contemporary Literature* 22 (1981) 121.

Intended represents all the good things Kurtz 'intended' to achieve; furthermore, she represents the best of all ideals, all the best which Kurtz has intended for himself, her and the world. She confesses "I knew him best." (Conrad 107) Marlow does not know whether this was the truth because for him it was just 'perhaps.' Marlow saw the atmosphere of the room, which was dark, compared to her "dark forehead." (Conrad 107) She is blind, and therefore cannot stand the truth. "Marlow has realised the need to save 'another soul' – the soul of civilization."[103] Kurtz's intentions were dead and entombed; that is why the Intended's house is described as being dead, cut-off, and hopelessly white; the house and the Intended embody the soul of civilization. In that last moment, Kurtz stares down into his intentions revealed by the wilderness, and he comes to terms with the wreckages of his life. Consequently, his heart beat to the wilderness and the primordial instincts of mankind and not to the civilizing mission. Betraying the soul of civilization, his soul has come to be possessed by the soul of the wilderness.

Marlow cannot tell the truth to the Intended and the whole world because they would be denied the opportunity to discover the truth for themselves. They have to struggle to get nearer and comprehend the basis of their existence and that is the reason why Marlow decides to lie; moreover, "the heavens do not fall for such a trifle." (Conrad 111) Robert Kimbrough states,

> The difference between Europe and Africa is the difference between two secondary symbols, the European woman who has helped to puff up Kurtz's pride and the African woman who has helped to deflate him. The Intended is totally protected, rhetorically programmed, nun-like in her adoration, living in black, in a place of darkness, in a pre-Eliot City of the Dead, in the wasteland of modern Europe...The Native Woman is Africa, all interior, in spite of her lavish mode of dress.[104]

To tell the Intended the truth would be to unleash horror and rape on the Intended's Europe because Marlow believes that "It's queer how out of touch with truth women are. They live in a world of their own...It is too beautiful altogether, and if they were to set it up it would go to pieces before the first sunset." (Conrad 18) The Victorian women in the story cannot understand the truth because they are simply not aware of

---

[103] Juliet McLauchlan, "The 'Value' and 'Significance' of *Heart of Darkness*", *Conradiana* 15 (1983) 8.
[104] Robert Kimbrough, *The World's Classics: Conrad, Joseph. 'Youth,' 'Heart of Darkness,' 'The End of the Tether,'* ed. and intro. Robert Kimbrough (Oxford: Oxford UP, 1984) 1-20.

reality. As a matter of fact, they are not even in touch with truth, which makes them redundant in a way, or at least not important for the development of the story, or even the world. "Oh, she is out of it – completely. They – the women I mean – are out of it – should be out of it. We must help them to stay in that beautiful world of their own, lest ours gets worse. Oh, she had to be out of it." (Conrad 69) Kurtz characterizes his fiancée and women in general as being apart from reality and truth; they live in a beautiful world of their own and have no notion of the things going on around them. They live in a kind of sphere and should be kept there in order not to interfere with man's seeking of truth. The Intended knew nothing about Kurtz, about his whereabouts, his mistress and so forth. She lied to herself and the whole world when she finally asked Marlow about Kurtz's last words; she wanted to hear what Marlow was going to say. She was ignorant of the truth around her, and the revelation of Kurtz's death would have killed her because she was not able to live with the truth; it would have simply spoiled her. "You knew what vast plans he had. I knew of them too – I could not perhaps understand – but others knew of them." (Conrad 109) She could not and did not understand him because they lived in different universes. Then she stretched out her arms to recollect the fake surface reality, her recollection of a man she once had known, and she then tried to understand but could not because of her futile existence. Nevertheless, she needed something to base her future life on, another lie that allowed her to continue to vegetate, "I want something to live with." (Conrad 110) Marlow did not tell her Kurtz's last words and betrayed therefore his desire for ultimate justice.

III.9. Kurtz's "Unspeakable Rites"

Stephen A. Reid suggests, "Kurtz's unspeakable rites and secrets concern human sacrifice and Kurtz consuming a portion of the sacrificial victim. Further, these sacrifices were established in the interest of perpetuating Kurtz's position as a man-god."[105] Following Sir George James Frazer, the natives believed that when their

---

[105] Stephen A. Reid, "The 'Unspeakable Rites' in *Heart of Darkness*," *Conrad: A Collection of Critical Essays. Twentieth Century Views*, ed. Marvin Mudrick (New Jersey: Prentice-Hall, 1966) 45.

"pontiff" was to die or fell ill he had to be replaced immediately, otherwise the earth would be annihilated as well.[106] Kurtz's position seems to have been different because he lost his strength "and thus we have the anomalous situation of the prolonged and acute anxieties of the natives and of Kurtz's continued power."[107] Reid has an interesting theory concerning Kurtz's maintenance of power because he believes that Kurtz, in order to revive his own strength and his credibility among the natives, took young man-gods and slew them. "These rites were perhaps annual, or were instituted with increasing frequency as Kurtz's illness became more frequent and pronounced. The heads on the poles were those of the victims; they faced Kurtz's hut."[108] Peter Firchow tells us about such rituals in his book *Envisioning Africa: Racism and Imperialism in Conrad's Heart of Darkness* when young people of the tribe were sacrificed by cutting off their heads. "The Russian was seen by the natives as an ultimate successor to the dying Kurtz,"[109] because he looked up to Kurtz and worshipped him as a god; as a result, he would have been the perfect replacement for Kurtz. Another remarkable feature, which could probably prove this theory, is the fact that Kurtz's mistress wanted to get rid of the Russian harlequin; moreover, she argued with Kurtz because she sensed that the Russian was likely to be the successor. They wanted Kurtz to stay with them and when he was taken away on the steamer, the native woman shouted in vain because she knew that Africa was not going to let him live after he had penetrated into the ultimate truth. Reid again suggests that the native woman "urged Kurtz to sacrifice himself for the good of the tribe."[110] Was Kurtz really going to sacrifice himself when Marlow discovered that the cabin was empty? It is a demanding question, but as Kurtz revealed, "I had immense plans...and now for this stupid scoundrel..." (Conrad 94), it is probable that he wanted to sacrifice himself for the sake of the tribe. Apparently the manager, the 'scoundrel,' had destroyed Kurtz's plans to enrich his power and wealth with ivory.

Why was he utterly lost? He was under a spell that had been emitted by a personified "wilderness that seemed to draw him to its pitiless breast by the awakening of the forgotten and brutal instincts, by the memory of gratified and monstrous passions...he had kicked himself loose on the earth...he had kicked the very earth to pieces." (Conrad 94-5) "But the wilderness had found him out early, and

---

[106] Sir George James Frazer, *The Golden Bough* (New York: Macmillan, 1960) 309.
[107] Reid, *Conrad: A Collection of Critical Essays. Twentieth Century Views* 47-8.
[108] Ibid. 48.
[109] Ibid. 49.
[110] Ibid. 50.

had taken on him a terrible vengeance for the fantastic invasion. I think it had whispered to him things about himself which he did not know...and the whisper had proved irresistibly fascinating. It echoed loudly within him because he was hollow at the core." (Conrad 83) Kurtz participates in rites he has no right to; his tribal ancestry in Europe does not allow him to join the natives because he has a different code within himself. Once this code is 'detribalised' he has to face ultimate destruction, but at the same time he was granted the unique but lethal opportunity to discover his true 'past' and that of humanity. "He has fallen into a vacant, amoral space between the European and African tribes because he belongs to both and yet to neither."[111] Kurtz knew that they would take him back to civilization and that therefore, all his influence would end there. As Marlow inferred his intelligence was perfectly clear but his soul became mad because he had seen himself exploiting those people; furthermore, he had realised the erroneousness of his report, and wanted to exterminate all those people like the manager and the pilgrims, who would continue dehumanising their ancestral world and origins. Reid goes on to illustrate that "Kurtz was forced into the rites and forced to continue them."[112] For Kurtz is was a trick to ensure his ascendancy within the tribe but as he became conscious of the manager's plan, he wanted to exterminate, first and foremost, the representative and the idea of the original brute, namely himself. When they took him away "Kurtz's life was running swiftly, too, ebbing, ebbing out of his heart into the sea of inexorable time." (Conrad 97) Marlow had only "peeped over the edge" and had seen the ultimate cause which "...was wide enough to embrace the whole universe, piercing enough to penetrate all the hearts that beat in the darkness." (Conrad 101) But we do not get any detailed account of the unspeakable rites because Conrad did not see anything like a ritual or sacrifice; he could only reconstruct what he had heard or read from others.

---

[111] Firchow, *Envisioning Africa* 120.

[112] Reid, *Conrad: A Collection of Critical Essays. Twentieth Century Views* 53.

III.10. Kurtz as the Harbinger of Light

Only Kurtz and Marlow experienced the temptation that befell both of them: to get one step further in understanding the mystery of their existence. What Kurtz did not know was the price he would have to pay for his glimpse. "Kurtz had arrived to the Congo with a notion of being considerably more than a mere producer of ivory. He believed that the whites were regarded by the savage natives as superior beings, and he meant to reform them. Instead of overcoming the savages' ignorance, however, Kurtz became one of them – as their demigod, to be true."[113] His intention was to return and perform great tasks as he claimed before his death "I'll carry my ideas out yet – I will return. I'll show you what can be done." (Conrad 88) In fact, Marlow comes to the conclusion that "I am Kurtz's friend – in a way...Mr Kurtz's reputation is safe with me. I did not know how truly I spoke." (Conrad 90) Later on he even goes one step further to announce, "I alone know how to mourn for him as he deserves." (Conrad 106) Why did he become one of them? He did not have to reform them because it was him and the other Europeans who had to be reformed and told that they were inferior to the natives. It was the white mission that would enrich the natives and bring them civilization; however, Kurtz clearly saw who was savage and therefore, became one of them, their demigod. "The horror, the horror" (Conrad 100) is the ultimate revelation of the hollowness of the white ivory, which shines on the outside, but is dark inside, and thereby points to a paradox at the heart of the Western civilisation.

> Hollowness everywhere, the hollowness typified in *Heart of Darkness* by the would-be Assistant Manager. It is a key image, connecting with a number of other 'hollownesses': the fire bucket with a hole in it, the manager's lack of entrails, the steamboat, resonant as a biscuit tin that carries the light bearers into darkest Africa. Above all, the ivory cranium of Kurtz, the hollow sham, for whom there remain only words without reference.[114]

Marlow strongly believes that telling the truth to the Intended "would have been too dark – too dark altogether..." (Conrad 111) That is Marlow's and Conrad's final statement about a study of Belgian colonialism and its unintelligible darkness in

---

[113] Adam Gillon, *Joseph Conrad. Twayne's English Authors Series*, ed. Kinley E. Roby (Boston: Twayne Publishers, 1982) 70.
[114] Mahood, *The Colonial Encounter* 18.

coping with the 'others.' Kurtz is left alone, and he is therefore free from the restraints of society. It is then that he discovers his freedom because "the discovery of the self is the discovery of one's freedom. The strong drives in human nature then emerge in all their force."[115] Kurtz rebels against the restrictions of civilized society such as the manager who plots against Kurtz, the brickmaker as the spy, and the hollow 'pilgrims' because they 'are not even alive;' on the contrary, Kurtz is attracted by the 'savage' reality of the jungle and makes a choice while the others cannot. His cry at the end is "a recoil from the whole mess of European rapacity and brutality in Africa into which he is being taken back."[116]

> Kurtz, who set out for Africa carrying the light of European civilization at its brightest, came face to face, like other post-Darwinian heroes before him, with the essential animal nature of man, over which civilization is mere clothing, and that then, with his typical ruthless honesty, he cast off his ideals and humanity and dared to live at the other extreme, as the total animal Darwin and the Naturalists said he really was; he tore down the façade behind which the other colonialists sheltered, and converted metaphor into brutal fact, not only devouring Africa, as they did, but, very specifically, devouring Africans...Daring to face the consequences of his nature, he loses his identity; unable to be totally beast and never again able to be fully human, he alternates between trying to return to the jungle and recalling in grotesque terms his former idealism.[117]

Kurtz was struggling between two extremes, the one denying the primal instincts and the other giving in to them. He wanted to join the rites for the last time and metaphorically speaking, ultimately become a native or a beast, but Marlow, who had had the possibility to catch a glimpse of the unknown side of life, rescued him and took him back to civilization; that is when Africa took his revenge on Kurtz and killed him. "But both the diabolic love and the unearthly hate of the mysteries it had penetrated fought for the possession of that soul satiated with primitive emotions, avid of lying fame, of sham distinction, of all the appearances of success and power." (Conrad 98) In the last moments of his life he struggles for what he has done, and Marlow pins it down when he relates "Did he live his life again in every detail of desire, temptation, and surrender during that supreme moment of complete knowledge?" (Conrad 99-100)

---

[115] Goonetilleke, *Joseph Conrad: Beyond Culture and Background* 79.
[116] Ibid. 82.
[117] E.N. Dorall, "Conrad and Coppola: Different Centres of Darkness," *Southeast Asian Review of English* 1(1980) 22-23.

III.11. Reactions to Conrad's Intention of *Heart of Darkness*

"*Heart of Darkness* projects the image of Africa as 'the other world,' the antithesis of Europe and therefore of civilization, a place where man's vaunted intelligence and refinement are really mocked by triumphant bestiality."[118] Achebe criticises Conrad's unwillingness to grant speech to the savages because they do not speak throughout the whole novel, with minor exceptions such as Kurtz's mistress. He goes on to call Conrad a racist and "...white racism against Africa is such a normal way of thinking that its manifestations go completely unremarked." Africa is depicted

> as setting and backdrop which eliminates the African as human factor. Africa as a metaphysical battlefield devoid of all recognizable humanity, into which the wandering European enters at his peril. Can nobody see the preposterous and perverse arrogance in thus rendering Africa to the role of props for the break-up of one petty European mind?...The real question is the dehumanisation of Africa and Africans which this age-long attitude has fostered and continues to foster in the world.[119]

Beyond any doubt, Achebe is right when he remarks that Conrad was obsessed with the word 'nigger' because he used it a lot. A possible explanation could be the influence of Victorianism and its morals as racism was on the agenda of the day and therefore, Conrad functioned as a mirror of its surroundings. "Conrad saw and condemned the evil of imperial exploitation but was strangely unaware of the racism on which it sharpened its iron tooth."[120] Patrick Brantlinger argues that *Heart of Darkness* "offers a powerful critique of at least some manifestations of imperialism and racism, as it simultaneously presents that critique in ways that can be characterised only as imperialist and racist...The novel itself...cancels out its own best intentions."[121] "In a world in which the truth that Marlow tells about civilized Europe is expressed through a lie, it is no wonder that Conrad claimed that fiction is nearer to truth than history."[122]

---

[118] Achebe, *The Massachusetts Review* 18 783.
[119] Ibid. 788.
[120] Ibid. 792.
[121] Patrick Brantlinger, *Rule of Darkness: British Literature and Imperialism, 1830-1914* (Ithaca: Cornell UP, 1988) 279, 295.
[122] Brook, *Case Studies in Contemporary Criticism. Joseph Conrad: 'Heart of Darkness,'* 242.

Conrad's main aim was to convey an image of Africa rather than to describe its geography, socio-economic conditions and inhabitants.

> The extraordinary power it has exercised and continues to exercise on its primarily Eurocentric audience resides in its confirmation of an already existing image or stereotype of Africa as the 'other,' as the imagined composite of all those things that white Eurocentrics most fear and abominate, especially in themselves – of the horror, in short. *Heart of Darkness* is about the deepest psychic fears in Conrad's and his readers' psyches.[123]

Conrad wrote in one of his letters "…it seems to me that the black man is deserving of as much humanization regard as any animal since he has nerves, feels pain, can be made physically miserable."[124] Watt admits, "Conrad habitually uses the derogatory racial terms which were general in the political and evolutionary thought of his time."[125] Achebe accused Conrad of not granting the natives the opportunity to speak, but instead they made "a violent babble of uncouth sounds."[126] David Deuby refers to Achebe's novel *Things Fall Apart* when he claims, "…Conrad certainly did not offer *Heart of Darkness* as a picture of the peoples of the Congo any more than Achebe's *Things Fall Apart*, set in a Nigerian village, purports to be a rounded picture of the British overlords."[127] Albert Schweitzer formulated an interesting thesis when he wrote about the Negro "…I am your brother, it is true, but your older brother."[128] It seems as if Conrad had the same notion about the natives; he considered them to be inferior to the extent that he was their older brother and the one who decided how to present them. "Albert Schweitzer, Charles Darwin, Alfred Wallace and T.H. Huxley all believed in the superiority of the whites. In the entry 'Negro' in the standard reference work of that time, the eleventh edition of the *Encyclopaedia Britannica*, it is unambiguously stated that 'mentally the Negro is inferior to the white' as well as to yellow races."[129] Furthermore, Conrad stated in his letters, "it is the difference between the races that I wanted to point out."[130] Marlow does understand what they

---

[123] Firchow, *Envisioning Africa* 23.
[124] Conrad, *The Collected Letters* 96.
[125] Ian Watt, *Conrad in the 19th Century* (Berkeley: California UP, 1979) 159.
[126] Chinua, Achebe. "An Image of Africa: Racism in Conrad's *Heart of Darkness*," *Joseph Conrad, 'Heart of Darkness*,' ed. Robert Kimbrough, 3rd ed. (New York: Norton 1988) 256-258.
[127] David Deuby, "Jungle Fever," *New Yorker* (Nov.6 1995) 127.
[128] Albert Schweitzer, *On the Edge of the Primeval Forest*, trans. C.T. Campion (London: A. and C. Black, 1924) 130.
[129] Firchow, *Envisioning Africa* 47.
[130] Conrad, *The Collected Letters* 94.

mean even if he does not understand what they say. He understands better than anyone else on board the riverboat what the significance is of all the cries they all hear as they approach Kurtz on their final journey. What is the function of language anyhow? Nature had spoken to Kurtz and had caressed him after having given him the possibility to look into himself and the nature of mankind. Marlow as well understands the cries of the natives because he recognizes their meaning: meaning is of vital importance for understanding while language resides on the surface of things. All the pilgrims, the manager who inspired "uneasiness" (Conrad 31), the brickmaker who caused Marlow to lie about his aunt's influence in Brussels, and the accountant do not comprehend the meaning of the natives, and the meaning of their journey into the 'heart of darkness;' they are guided by greed and ignorance. The only one who seems to have been influenced superficially was the Russian; "…this man enlarged my mind. He opened his arms wide, staring at me with his little blue eyes that were perfectly round." (Conrad 78) The key-figures in the story all open their arms to symbolize the great energy and influence that penetrates them from Kurtz and the nature behind him. The Russian represents also an outlet for Kurtz and his message, and in opening up his arms he spreads the all-pervading revelation of the truth. The doctor in Brussels tells Marlow, "…the changes take place inside…" (Conrad 17) Language distinguishes humans from animals and "…Conrad's remark about having been a mere animal before going to the Congo may be further interpreted to mean that only those who are fully conscious of their linguistic status and power are to be considered fully human…if Conrad is a racist, it is in this 'weak' or surface sense only."[131] Frances B. Singh states, "He may sympathise with the plight of blacks, he may be disgusted by the effects of economic colonialism, but because he has no desire to understand or appreciate people of any culture other than his own, he is not emancipated from the mentality of a colonizer."[132]

Their languages are different but the meaning stays the same in all languages; nevertheless, it is only Marlow who grasps their meaning.

---

[131] Firchow, *Envisioning Africa* 61.
[132] Singh, *Conradiana* 45.

IV. *Things Fall Apart*
IV.1. The Life and Works of Chinua Achebe

Chinua Achebe was born in 1930 in the village of Ogidi, one of the first centres of Anglican missionary work in Igboland, Eastern Nigeria. His background is Christian, for his father Isaiah Okafor Achebe was one of the first Igbo men to become connected with a mission. Thus, the writer was exposed to both worlds, that of the Igbo, the second largest tribal group in South Eastern Nigeria, and that of the European Christians. Because of his father's position and the fact that he himself attended the Church Missionary Society's village school headed by his father, Achebe was excluded from certain activities that other village children participated in, and this made him aware of 'differences' in approaches to life.

He was educated at the Government College in Umuahia, beginning in 1944, and then went on to become one of the first students to be graduated from the University College at Ibadan in 1953. Although he entered the university to study medicine, Achebe was attracted to the liberal arts and later decided to read English literature. Achebe did retain an interest in Nigeria, however, and in 1954 he began work for the Nigerian Broadcasting Company in Lagos. He has also been interested in the field of publishing throughout his career. In 1958 he became the Founding Editor of Heinemann Educational Books' "African Writers Series."[133] Besides being Director of Heinemann in Nigeria, Achebe has been Director of the Nwankwo-Ifejika publishing house, has been a Foundation member of the Society of Nigerian Authors, served as an Editorial Advisor for the "African Writers Series" from 1962 until 1972, was the chairman of Citadel Books, Ltd., in 1967, and has been a member of the East Central State Library Board since 1971.

By 1966 Achebe had advanced to the position of Director of External Broadcasting for Nigeria, an appointment that led to travel throughout Africa and America. But with the outbreak of the civil war in 1966, the massacre of Igbos in Northern Nigeria, and the secession of the Eastern Region under the name of Biafra, Achebe relinquished his post. He had narrowly escaped confrontation with armed soldiers who apparently believed that his novel, *A Man of the People*, implicated him

---

[133] with his own *Things Fall Apart* being the first volume published in the series - there are now five titles listed under his name.

in Nigeria's first military coup. When he returned to the Eastern Region, Achebe intended to embark on another publishing venture with other young Igbos, among them the promising poet Christopher Okigbo, who was killed later that same year. Achebe's career as a university academic began in 1967 with his appointment as Senior Research Fellow at the University of Nigeria. He was made Emeritus Professor in 1985. Since the end of the war, Achebe has primarily been involved in university teaching in Nigeria and in the United States, at North Western University, the University of Massachusetts, the University of Connecticut, and most recently, at the City University of New York (1989).

Among his awards and honours, Achebe lists the Margaret Wrong Memorial Prize (1959) for *Things Fall Apart*, the 1960 Nigerian National Trophy, a Rockefeller Fellowship (1960-1961), a UNESCO Fellowship (1963), the New Statesman's Jock Campbell award in 1965 for *Arrow of God*, an appointment as Senior Research Fellow at the University of Nigeria at Nsukka since 1967, honorary Doctor of Letters from Dartmouth College (1972), the University of Southampton (1975), and the University of Ife (1978), a D. Univ. from the University of Stirling (1975), a Doctor of Laws from the University of Prince Edward Island (1976), an honorary Doctor of Humane Letters degree from the University of Massachusetts in 1978, the Commonwealth Poetry Prize in 1974, the Lotus Award for Afro-Asian Writers in 1975, and election as an Honorary Fellow to the Modern Language Association in 1973 and as a Neil Gunn fellow by the Scottish Arts Council in 1975. Most recently, in 1987, he received Nigeria's highest award for intellectual achievement, the Nigerian National Merit Award.

Achebe is the author of many novels, short stories, essays and children's books. *Things Fall Apart*, his first novel, was published in 1958. It has sold over eight million copies, and has been translated into at least 45 languages. It was followed by *No Longer at Ease* (1960), then *Arrow of God* (1964), which won the first New Statesman Jock Campbell Prize, and *A Man of the People* (1966). *Anthills of the Savannah* was shortlisted for the Booker McConnell Prize in 1987. *Beware Soul Brother*, a book of poetry, won the Commonwealth Poetry Prize in 1972.

Achebe lives in the USA, teaching at Bard College. He is married and has four children.

IV.2. Introduction to *Things Fall Apart*

In three parts the book tells the story of Ogbuefi Okonkwo, an Igbo tribesman who is very much a participant in the traditional life of his people. As the novel opens, the white man with his new religion has not yet appeared, and Achebe skilfully draws a picture of the full life of the village, complete with its social codes and gods. Early colonialism and the import of Christianity bring destruction to the tribe's traditional way of life, however, and *Things Fall Apart* is the story of an individual trying to turn aside the powerful new forces of Christianity and a foreign system of government. Ironically, the conflict leads to Okonkwo's isolation from both his traditional society and the new one that is replacing it. As an old warrior whose prowess was once legendary, Okonkwo makes one final effort to impress upon his people the truths of life and to defeat the encroaching European world, but his personal tragedy is symbolic of the society-wide conflict and as a symbol he is doomed. The novel ends with Okonkwo's suicide.

IV.3. Igbo History from 1860 to 1900

The first missionaries settled among the Igbo in Onitsha in 1857,[134] but had arrived almost two decades before, under the auspices of the Niger Expedition, equipped by the British government for trade. The expedition was commissioned in London in 1840 and two missionaries who were already working with the freed slaves in Sierra Leone were selected to join the expedition.

The long isolation of the mysterious West African hinterland was ended in the 19th century following the discovery of the true course of the Niger by adventurous British explorers. Almost simultaneously with the European penetration of the West African hinterland, the Christian Missions were endeavouring to make good their long neglect

---

[134] the following information about the historical situation of Nigeria and the Igbos is taken from Elisabeth Isichei, *The Ibo People and the Europeans: The Genesis of a Relationship to 1906* (London: Faber and Faber, 1973) 72-181. and Nicholas Ibeawuchi Omenka, *The School in the Service of Evangelisation: The Catholic Educational Impact in Eastern Nigeria 1886-1950. Studies on Religion in Africa VI* (Leiden: E.J. Brill, 1989) 11-28.

of the Africans in their missionary enterprise. The Berlin Conference held in 1885 granted freedom of navigation on the Niger and the Congo, and assigned the responsibility of protecting the subjects and establishment of the European nations on the Niger to Britain. A diplomatic convention signed in Paris on June 14, 1898 made Britain the sole master of the Niger Countries.

The most numerous and influential ethnic group in Eastern Nigeria are the Igbo. They are at the same time the second largest national unit in the whole of Nigeria and are found on both sides of the Niger. The Igbo had no kingdoms or powerful city-states like the other major tribes of Nigeria. Until the 19th century, they lived in self-governing and democratic villages. The main centres of Igbo population east of the Niger are Owerri, Orlu, Umuahia, Onitsha, Enugu, and parts of the Abakiliki and Port Harcourt provinces. The Igbo are primarily farmers and enterprising businessmen. Igboland was the centre of Catholic missionary and educational endeavours in Nigeria in the 19th and 20th centuries. If they exhibited a national tendency towards Catholicism, it was perhaps because, of all the Christian denominations, the Catholics best satisfied their propensity to seek external influences – better education, more profound liturgy, ample opportunity for contact with the white man.

The typical Igbo state was a small, democratic society, with an intricate system of political institutions where the voice of elders generally predominated, and with much scope for individual mobility. Many were grouped into clans, or tribes, united by the agnatic charter of a common ancestor. The Igboland was characterized by the activity of its economic life and the vast number of its markets with the yam as the central crop. Igboland consisted of a large number of small independent states with important institution such as the oracle. The basic structure of the Igbo religion was a supreme God and a host of lesser divinities and spirits for the daily affairs of men. When the Christian missions penetrated into the Nigerian hinterland, the rulers welcomed missions and trade but the initial welcome was succeeded by a period of prosecution, as traditional rulers realised that missionary teaching tended to undermine the customs of their society, and perhaps challenge their own authority. Converts were drawn from the lowest strata of society. Those marginal men and women, who had little hope from existing structures because they were treated like outcasts, could only gain from a new system of values and ideals. Relationships between the missionaries and the Igbo people deteriorated because the middle years of the 19th century were an age of anxiety. The first encounter of the Niger peoples with colonialism meant the systematic subordination of their interests to the economic interests of a foreign power. It meant the repeated experience of the violence by which this foreign power maintained its authority.

In 1905, a doctor, travelling by a bicycle in the Ahiara area, was put to death, and his death, as always, was expiated in numerous, though uncounted, Igbo lives. The death of a single European, at the hands of those whose country was being conquered by his compatriots, was a brutal murder. The death of scores of Igbos, defending their native land with machetes and muzzle loaders in the face of machine guns, was a good bag of the enemy. The Igbo people resisted colonial conquest with courage, and sometimes with contemporary success. As a matter of fact, the enormous disparity in armaments and in state resources meant that the contest was a hopelessly unequal one. The preservation of law and order on behalf of the Europeans had two main aspects. The first was the suppression of conflict between the Igbo groups and the second the suppression of practices which the British considered inhuman – human sacrifice, infanticide, and slavery. Igbo resistance to the spread of colonial rule was never a uniform phenomenon. Some did not resist when colonial rule was first imposed, but did so after a time, when its true significance was more apparent. Some wished to resist, but were dissuaded by the fate of their neighbours. Others decided that their interests were best served, not by resisting the new power, but by co-operating with it. The most common solution was perhaps that of eclecticism – a personal synthesis of elements of the old and new.

IV.4. The Igboland and its Inhabitants

Chinua Achebe stated that Nigerians would all describe Igbo people

> as aggressive, arrogant and clannish. The Igbo culture being receptive to change, individualistic and highly competitive, gave the Igbo man an unquestioned advantage over his compatriots in securing credentials for advancement in Nigerian colonial society. This kind of creature, fearing nor God no man, was custom-made, to grasp the opportunities, such as they were, of the white man's dispensation.[135]

---

[135] Chinua Achebe, *The Trouble with Nigeria* (Oxford: Heinemann Educational Publishers, 1983) 45-6.

The Igbo people were therefore very self-confident and also open to new influences because the most important part of their culture was the actual clan although the society was highly individual as represented by Okonkwo; that is the reason why Achebe talks about clannishness within the culture. Another remarkable trait of the Igbo people and especially Okonkwo is hubris: he may not be aware of the fact that he risks his own life and that of others by behaving like he does. He loves the people around him and he knows that but he is, after all, afraid of showing his female or weaker element of his being to the other tribe members and especially his family. "He had no patience with unsuccessful men. He had no patience with his father."[136] Achebe goes on to say that "the rise of the Igbo in Nigerian affairs was due to the self-confidence engendered by their open society and their belief that one man is as good as another, that no condition is permanent."[137] Once the white man started to foster and welcome those members of the Igbo society who had been primarily treated as outcasts or those who had had the slightest doubt about the traditional way of life of the tribe, it was a comparatively easy task for the Christian missionaries to complete their duty in splitting up the tribe so that the old customs would fall apart and crumble to pieces. "The trouble with Nigeria is simply and squarely a failure of leadership...The Nigerian problem is the unwillingness or inability of its leaders to rise to the responsibility, to the challenge of personal example which are the hallmarks of true leadership."[138]

Carroll David describes the Igbo territory and customs as follows:

> The territory of the Igbo in Southeastern Nigeria stretches from the low-lying swampland of the Niger Delta through the tableland of the centre of the region to the northern hill country of Onitsha. The social structure of the Igbo tribe consists of countless small local communities. Within the village itself power is dispersed among various groups, and social equilibrium is maintained by a complex system of checks and balances. A law only establishes itself gradually by village consensus. The Igbo culture is a title society which plays a dominant role in the affairs of the community, lays down rules of conduct for their members, and above all, creates a source of unity by accepting the titled from other villages.[139]

---

[136] Chinua Achebe, *Things Fall Apart* (Oxford: Heinemann, 1958) 3. Further references to the book will be made with parenthetical documentation.
[137] Achebe, *The Trouble with Nigeria* 47.
[138] Ibid. 1.
[139] David Carroll, *Chinua Achebe: Novelist, Poetic, Critic* (London: Macmillan, 1980) 13-4.

The first contact with the Europeans was at the end of the 19th century. A system of direct rule was consequently imposed in 1900 by dividing the territory into areas to be controlled by 'native courts' presided over by British district commissioners with certain chosen Igbo members. In 1918 the District Commissioner was removed and a system of local government imposed. After having invaded the territory of Nigeria, the British colonial masters "found a people, highly decentralised, segmented and in an advanced level of republicanism...The fundamental social unit was patrilineal, and each unit occupied a compound made up of several sub patriarchal units."[140] When the Europeans came with their mission to bring Christianity and civilization to the peoples of Nigeria, they once again widened the gulf between the two already different cultures because they believed "in the superiority of Europe and the existence of lower races."[141] The tragedy of that belief is the final defeat and resulting destruction of the natives' way of life. Therefore, Blant calls it "'Eurocentric diffusionism': Europeans are seen as the makers of history. Europe eternally advances, progresses, modernizes. The rest of the world advances more sluggishly, or stagnates: it is traditional society. Therefore, the world has a geographical centre and a permanent periphery: an Inside and an Outside. Inside leads and Outside lags. Inside innovates, Outside imitates."[142]

Things Fall Apart is a vision of what life was like in Igboland at the end of 1900. Chinua Achebe portrays a beautiful picture of the Igbo society and their customs at that time, and in doing so, he creates a realistic recollection of a past that was to be forgotten after the white man had destroyed the harmony. "Umuofia is portrayed as a pluralistic society, which admires energetic, aggressive and ambitious members, one that is patient, tolerant and forbearing, entrenched in the wisdom of its ancients, yet flexible and adaptable when necessary."[143] Ravenscroft observes that through Achebe's vivid presentation of the elaborate rituals of the society's life, "the impression emerges of a carefully ordered, yet flexible culture, communal in nature

---

[140] Benedict Chiaka Njoku, *The Four Novels of Chinua Achebe: A Critical Study, American University Studies* (New York: Peter Lang, 1984) 14.
[141] Alastair Pennycock, *English and the Discourses of Colonialism* (London: Routledge, 1998) 47.
[142] J.M. Blant, *The Colonizer's Model of the World: Geographical Diffusionism and Eurocentric History* (New York: The Guildford Press, 1993) 1.
[143] Umelo Ojinmah, *Chinua Achebe: New Perspectives* (Nigeria: Spectrum Books Limited, 1991) 13.

yet allowing for a considerable measure of individuality."[144] Achebe never condemns Christianity and he does not even condemn individual missionaries. "What he deplores is their total ignorance of the people to whom they were preaching, their uninformed assumptions that Africans did not have any concept of God and their lack of any self-knowledge which might have made them question something of their own motives in desiring to see themselves as bringers of salvation."[145] Speed Diana calls *Things Fall Apart* "a piece of history; the reader feels the calamity on every page of the impending collapse of an ancient, self-reliant, purposeful and organised society in which the individual personality is not an end in itself but a contribution to the whole. This was not one village nor even one tribe, but an Africa that is already extinct in the minds of the present generation."[146]

IV.5. Achebe's Language and Style

Achebe is a postcolonial writer who tries to come to terms with his own past, namely, that of the Igbo people in Nigerian at the end of the 19th century when the white man invaded Nigeria. "The ex-colonial writer is consistently ambivalent towards the metropolitan tongue. On the one hand, it is the historical tool with which his colonial status was shaped and the indigenous traditions of his 'jungle' distorted. And, on the other hand, this alien tongue is the useful lingua franca through which he reaches his discrete readership in Europe and Africa."[147] Generally speaking, the white man's failure to understand African customs in *Things Fall Apart* is linked with his ignorance of the African's language. When it comes to criticism and understanding of the language, Achebe claims "We are not opposed to criticism but we are getting a little weary of all the special types of criticism which have been designed for us by people whose knowledge of us is very limited. No man can

---

[144] Arthur Ravenscroft, *Chinua Achebe,* ed. Ian Scott-Kilvert (London: Longman, Green & Co, 1969) 16.
[145] Margaret Lawrence, *Long Drums and Cannons: Nigerian Dramatists and Novelists 1952-1966* (London: Macmillan, 1968) 106-7.
[146] Diana Speed, "Review of *Things Fall Apart*," *Black Orpheus* 5 (1959) 52.
[147] Lloyd W. Brown, "Cultural Norms and Modes of Perception in Achebe's Fiction," *Critical Perspectives on Nigerian Literatures*, ed. Bernth Lindfors (Washington: Three Continent Press, 1976) 132.

understand another whose language he does not speak."[148] According to Mercer Cook, "taking the white man's language, dislocating his syntax, recharging his words with new strength and sometimes with new meaning before hurling them back in his teeth, while upsetting his self-righteous complacency and clichés, our poets rehabilitate such terms as Africa and blackness, beauty and peace."[149]

The story is told by a seemingly wise, compassionate and sympathetic elder, who is ably conversant with Igbo world-view, philosophy and culture. He is aware of the past and of the intrusion of Christianity and European cultures. It is a 3rd person narrative, but there is no suggestion of an omniscient observer analysing the customs and habits of the Igbo community. The language of the people of Umuofia is full of Igbo proverbs, which try to solve everyday problems with traditional wisdom. "If the nub of a contemporary situation can be seen to correspond to the generalised truth contained in a proverb, then present perplexity and past experience are made congruent, and language remains an effective instrument for coping with life."[150] The proverbs serve to justify the way of life of the Igbo clan and range from the important events of a man's life and bride price to war and marriage such as "he who brings kola, brings life," (Achebe 5) "if a child washed his hands he could eat with kings," (Achebe 6) "when mother cow is chewing grass its young ones watch its mouth," (Achebe 50) "as a man danced so the drums were beaten for him" (Achebe 133) and many more. The proverbs are drawn from nature indicating the connection between human life and the soil. As Achebe puts it himself "Among the Igbo the art of conversation is regarded very highly, and proverbs are the palm oil with which words are eaten." (Achebe 5) As a matter of fact, Achebe's proverbs can serve as a key to an understanding of his novel because "he uses them to sound and reiterate themes, to sharpen characterisation, to clarify conflict, and to focus on the values of the society he is portraying."[151] The proverbs, similes and stories such as the one with the ear and the mosquito, or the one with the birds and the tortoise help to evoke the cultural milieu in which the action takes place. An outstanding example is that of Okonkwo's chi: he is portrayed as a wrestler and he believes that "when a man says yes his chi says yes also. Okonkwo said yes very strongly; so his chi agreed. And not only his

---

[148] Chinua Achebe, "Where Angels Fear to Tread," *Nigeria Magazine* 75 (1962) 61-2.
[149] Mercer Cook, and Stephen E. Henderson, *African Voices of Protest: Militant Black Writer in Africa and the United States* (Wisconsin: Madison, 1969) 52.
[150] G.D. Killam, *The Writings of Chinua Achebe* (London: Heinemann, 1969) 15.
[151] Bernth Lindfors, "The Palm Oil with which Achebe's Words Are Eaten," *African Literature Today* 1 (1968) 6.

chi but his clan too, because it judged a man by the work of his hands." (Achebe 19) The adversary is not the white man, but rather Okonkwo's chi. "His chi and his clan say no but he believes the opposite and the chaos is unleashed. All the proverbs reveal that no one, least of all Okonkwo himself, considers oneself an ordinary mortal; rather, he is the sort of man who would dare to wrestle with his chi."[152] The use of proverbs highlights the cultural values of the Igbo society before infiltration of the white man. "Igbo society's desire for advancement, to induce spirituality against any excess of materialism, self-criticism, are a reminder of the adaptability of the Igbo society to a changing world."[153] To emphasise the exclusivity of the two worlds, Achebe often leaves Igbo words untranslated; they refer to the sheer impossibility to compare the two different worlds with their opposite sets of values. There are a variety of words such as *iba*, Enzinma's fever which can be identified with malaria; *ogbanje*, a child who repeatedly dies and returns to its mother to be reborn; *egwugwu*, a masquerader who impersonates one of the ancestral spirits of the village; *obi*, the large living quarters of the head of the family, and many more. "The reference to a possible doubt among the women spectators advertises the distance of the narration from faith in the world it describes."[154]

IV.6. Okonkwo: Society's Offspring and Lonely Wrestler

Okonkwo is the product of his society for his behaviour reflects the demands of his society. In a way, his surroundings are also responsible for the final outbreak of violence because traditional Igbo society always stresses the manly qualities of life in general; yams are equal to fame because "yam stood for manliness," (Achebe 24) and being a great warrior means being accepted. His father Unoka was a failure because he was "in fact a coward and could not bear the sight of blood." (Achebe 5) On the contrary, Okonkwo is one of the most important men in Umuofia because "he was a

---

[152] Lindfors, *African Literature Today* 9.
[153] Arthur Kemoli, *An H.E.B. Student's Guide: Notes on Chinua Achebe's 'Things Fall Apart'* (Nairobi: Heinemann, 1975) 6.
[154] Neil Ten Kortenaar, "How the Centre is Made To Hold in *Things Fall Apart*," *Postcolonial Literatures: Achebe, Ngugi, Desai, Walcott*, eds. Michael Parker and Roger Starkey (New York: St. Martin's, 1995) 38.

man of action, a man of war...In Umuofia's latest war he was the first to bring home a human head." (Achebe 8) Once again, human heads are a symbol of power and achievement according to which one's position within the tribe is established.

> If he is plagued by fear of failure and of weakness, it is because his society puts such premium on success; if he is obsessed with status it is because his society is preoccupied with rank and prestige; if he is always itching to demonstrate his prowess in war it is because his society reveres bravery and courage, and measures success by the numbers of human heads a man has won; if he is contemptuous of weaker men it is because his society has conditioned him into despising cowards. Okonkwo is the personification of his society's values, and is determined to succeed in this rat-race.[155]

After reading this passage, one is immediately reminded of *Heart of Darkness* and Kurtz's heads on the poles. Human heads are an indication of manly prowess and success; it is society that rewards those who kill for the benefit of the community and the tribe as a whole. "The tragedy of Okonkwo originates from his resistance to change, from his imperviousness to the allurements of modernism born of European cultural traits. Christianity and European culture repudiated African laws and customs, all manner of social cohesiveness and solidarity was disrupted."[156] Okonkwo does not expect his surroundings to be a paradise of eternal peace when the Europeans finally invade his territory, "nor is he dreaming of a Golden Age in the far-off past when the Africans dwelt in undisturbed utopian peace and ease. But in the Igbo society of his dreams father and son, men and women enjoyed common beliefs, common liturgies, common value system and simple expectations."[157] Okonkwo is the proud warrior. Okonkwo identifies the Europeans as a source of destruction: "the white man is going to become a social, political and cultural abomination to the people of Umuofia, the agent of destruction, just as locusts are agents of destruction."[158] The European mentality robs the free spirit of the Africans of their individuality and liberty of thought. The colonizers are depraved in their perception of cultures, languages, and customs different from their own due to their ignorant view of the 'other;' they do not want to accept the individual, personal, and private identity of their "enemy" and therefore, transform "his/her psyche and

---

[155] Eustace Palmer, *An Introduction to the African Novel* (London: Heinemann, 1972) 53.
[156] Benedict Chiaka Njoku, *The Four Novels of Chinua Achebe: A Critical Study*, American University Studies (New York: Peter Lang, 1984) 18.
[157] Njoku, *The Four Novels of Chinua Achebe* 24-5.
[158] Ibid. 27.

Weltanschauung...He sees Western civilization and Christianity as productive of polarizing influences, which are the cause of things falling apart...Okonkwo is not running away from spiritual intimacy and cultural blending, but from total absorption which seeks to have no room for the cultural realities of thousands of years gone by."[159] But in the whole confusing impact of the whites on Umuofia one element could not be taken apart from another. "They have their perplexingly subversive religion, they have their total ignorance of the very meaning of tradition and reverence, they have physical force on a scale that makes them inaccessible to reason; they are in fact mere anarchy let loose on the Umuofian world."[160] Okonkwo finally comes to terms with his defeat and prepares for his last mission as one of the greatest warriors of his tribe: "Ok finally realising that the past had been defeated, withdraws, and splendid in his finest warrior's raiment, with a more than Roman dignity, puts himself to death, achieving with his final stroke the heroic status which the treacheries of time had forbidden him even during the most successful phases of his life."[161] The tragedy of Okonkwo's death is the result of the collapse of the whole tribe. "He...was hurled to catastrophe as much by his own folly as by the alien forces over which he had no control."[162]

IV.7. The Second Coming

"Turning and turning in the widening gyre
The falcon cannot hear the falconer;
Things fall apart; the centre cannot hold;
Mere anarchy is loosed upon the world." (Achebe 1)

The title *Things Fall Apart* refers to the Yeatsian prophecy of the decline and fall of the current incarnation of the West. The title stems from *The Second Coming* of W.B. Yeats, the connection between the theme of the book and Yeats' vision of

---

[159] Ibid. 32-5.
[160] A.G. Stock, "Yeats and Achebe," *Journal of Commonwealth Literature* 5 (1968) 110.
[161] William Walsh, *A Manifold Voice: Studies in Commonwealth Literature* (London: Chatto and Windus, 1970) 52.
[162] Ali G. Morty, "Review of *Things Fall Apart*," *Black Orpheus* 6 (1959) 49.

history as a succession of civilizations, each giving way to another. The world of freedom and peace is overrun by a supposedly superior civilization with the aim of bringing the torch of light to the darkness. The Christian missionaries try to undermine the natives' belief in their gods by claiming their nullity; at the same time their effort is directed at the outcasts of society in order to win them over and to create a basis to defeat the hardliners. Achebe is using the Yeatsian idea as an instrument to analyse and interpret human experience in a confrontation between different ways of life. "Okonkwo has imposed a rigid code of aloofness upon his generous human impulses and magnified it into a principle of right conduct."[163] The exile represents a dramatic cut in his carrier, as he was to achieve one of the highest titles of the tribe. Okonkwo made a terrible mistake and he killed the boy at the dead man's funeral. The village decides to send him on a seven-year exile to the village of his mother; once again, Okonkwo must face the female side of his life by being sent to his mother's clan, which is considered weak and sustaining. Simultaneously, he hates "everything his father Unoka had loved. One of those things was gentleness and another was idleness." (Achebe 10) His stay in Mbanta proves to be fatal for his life and that of his family as Christianity sneaked into Umuofia and ripped away his own son Nwoye. "Achebe implies throughout that Okonkwo is no mere automative victim of a social setting which encourages the qualities he has cultivated. He does have the power of choice. Nor is Okonkwo a victim of history, Okonkwo's fall has also been seen as the inevitable outcome of his own self-forged steeling of the gentler impulses."[164]

The Yeatsian poem draws our attention simultaneously to the forces of nature at work because the life of the Igbo people seems to be governed by the seasons. In the first part Achebe romantically describes the life of the clan to then go on to prepare for the ultimate change of season. I will call it the season of physical and psychological change, which turns the life of the villagers upside down. The coming of the white man is compared to the descent of the locusts, which "ate up all the wild grass in the fields." (Achebe 39) Those insects descend on the fields and destroy everything; the same thing applies to the missionaries and the colonizer in general. They came to the unknown and without trying to apprehend the differences between their own culture and that of Africa, they systematically forced the Africans to adopt their values and understanding of the world. The locusts destroy and nature can

---

[163] Ravenscroft, *Chinua Achebe* 11.
[164] Ibid. 15.

reproduce its beauty but the white man has rooted out any opportunity to revive the old customs. Therefore, the Igbo people compare the white man with "leper, and the polite name for leprosy was 'the white skin.'" (Achebe 53) The albino on the iron horse was killed but he had only been the messenger, the harbinger of the locusts who would invade the territory and leave behind them traces of destruction. "Achebe is a 20th century Igbo man, a de-colonized writer, and recognizes the wide gulf which exists between his present day society and that of Igbo villagers of 60 years ago."[165] Yeats envisions human history as a succession of gyres, of cycles, which prepare humanity for the coming of Christ, and the Christian phase will be followed in turn by another cycle, by another coming which will change life dramatically. Therefore, Achebe creates the picture of 19th century Africa, which is followed by Europeanization, another era.

> The very parallels between Yeats and Achebe are a source of irony, for they touch upon those characteristic tensions, which govern the relationship between the ex-colonial writer and the metropolitan culture. Yeats's subject, history, and the rich association of past events which the poet evokes trough the Judaeo-Christian symbols of the 'first coming' – all belong to that era of human experience and understanding from which the myths of Christian Europe have always excluded the African. Namely, in evoking Yeats's themes, Achebe implies that the sense of history and tradition, the burdens of cultural continuity, decay and rebirth, have all been the African's lot as well as the Westerner's. Achebe uses the literary traditions of the English tongue to liberate the African's identity and history from the 'ethnocentric images that have been enshrined in the psychopathology of the colonizer's language.[166]

IV.8. The Female Vein: Okonkwo's Manliness and Refusal of his Feminine Side

The female principle always acted as a restraint on the male world in order to keep it in balance. But as a matter of fact, when Okonkwo and his family are exiled to Mbanto, Uchendu tries to explain to Okonkwo that the female principle and the 'mother' is a decisive part in the life of the Igbos because "your mother is there to protect you. She is buried there. And that is why we say that mother is supreme."

---

[165] Killam, *The Writings of Chinua Achebe* 14.
[166] Brown, *Critical Perspectives on Nigerian Literatures* 135-137.

(Achebe 97) Okonkwo does not realise that in order to balance his life, he has to listen to his female voice to be able to establish his existence. "Igbo society has always been materialistic. This may sound strange because Igbo life had at the same time a strong spiritual dimension controlled by gods, ancestors, personal spirits/chi. The success of the culture was the balance between the two...Today we have kept the materialism and thrown away the spirituality which should keep it in check."[167] Okonkwo kills himself and consequently becomes what he tried to avoid all his life: the follower of his father because he can not be cut down from the tree by his fellow villagers, but only by the white soldiers after the District Commissioner clears the scene. He plans to reduce this incident to another unimportant, silly and little chapter in the great book of white civilization, another tragic incident on the way to a better world. "The dangling body of Okonkwo is merely an undignified detail to the District Commissioner who has him cut down and the indifference displayed by him is symptomatic not only of the utter failure of the two systems to understand each other but, through the irony of the final paragraph, symptomatic of the hypocritical basis of the imperial-colonial notion of the civilizing mission, the idea contained in the phrase 'the white man's burden.'"[168]

It is Okonkwo's refusal to accept his feminine side and that of the whole philosophy behind Igbo culture that sets off the drama at the end, and Obierika states ferociously, "That man was one of the greatest men in Umuofia. You drove him to kill himself; and now he will be buried like a dog..." (Achebe 149) Another episode which demonstrates Okonkwo's fear to acknowledge his weaker side is the one with Ikemefuma: Achebe illustrates how Okonkwo's inherent fear of being like his father, of being thought weak and effeminate, leads him to excesses, even to kill the boy though he was very fond of him – "inwardly of course. Okonkwo never showed any emotion openly...To show affection was a sign of weakness; the only thing worth demonstrating was strength." (Achebe 20) In the end the oracle decides to kill the boy but not without warning him not to participate; Okonkwo ignores the warning and kills him. He cannot allow himself to assemble his own father, but "it is the kind of action for which the goddess wipes out whole families." (Achebe 47) Given the nature of Umuofia's cultural heritage, "...a culture where the line of division between the dead, the living, and the unborn is shown to be so thin as to be almost non-existent, where their symbiotic interaction helps maintain the cosmic cyclical balance

---

[167] Achebe, *African Writers on African Writing* 179.
[168] Killam, *The Writings of Chinua Achebe* 32.

of the Igbo world-view, Okonkwo's relationship to his father, which continued even after the man's death, though pragmatic, is nonetheless unwise."[169] Okonkwo's behaviour towards the members of his family becomes increasingly intolerable because he does not know anymore where to draw the line between his manliness and futile violence. "At the height of his achievements and on the verge of achieving greater glories, the gods singled him out for humiliation and destruction."[170] Okonkwo was not a cruel man but he could not show it because "his whole life was dominated by fear, the fear of failure and of weakness." (Achebe 9) He rules his household very severely without sometimes knowing when to stop mistreating them. He beats his youngest wife Ojiugo during the Week of Peace, or nearly shots his second wife Ekwefi because she dared to doubt his skills. "Ok persistently shows an aversion to the female side on which the society's survival depends, and it is this that leads to the tragedy. In Achebe's view, Okonkwo's established deviation from his society and the fact that most of his excesses were already manifest before he ever comes in contact with any European, indicate abuse of both power and responsibility."[171] In order to justify himself, his single-mindedness develops into egocentricity, until he is not able anymore to distinguish between madness and right conduct. "His insistence on manliness is such that he becomes a menace to his society even within the limits of its code. Ok has had to steel himself against ordinary human feelings, so that he becomes dehumanised. His son is the antithesis of his father; there is an Oedipus touch to the relationship of Nwoye with his father."[172] Nwoye is different from the other villagers and develops an antipathy against certain customs within society such as the casting away of twins. At first "Okonkwo was inwardly pleased at his son's development, and he knew it was due to Ikemefuma." (Achebe 37) The essence of the story becomes clear when his father kills Ikemefuma, the boy from the other village and Nwoye's best friend; even Okonkwo treats him like his own son. But his rigid code and the fear of being thought weak and not capable of fulfilling his duty leads him to kill the boy. That is when Nwoye turns away from his father and reduces Okonkwo to the role of his own father, Unoka. "His defection to Christianity later on has a double significance – it is at the same time an act of revolt

---

[169] Ibid. 20.
[170] Koofi Awoonor, *The Breast of the Earth* (New York: Anchor Press, 1976) 264.
[171] Ojinmah, *Chinua Achebe: New Perspectives* 24.
[172] Irele Abiola, *Introduction to African Literature: An Anthology of Critical Writing*, ed. Ulli Beier (London: Longman, 1967) 179.

against his father as well as a rejection of the society that he embodied."[173] Nwoye is called Isaac: "Achebe draws an unforced and unexplained deeply ironic parallel between Okonkwo and the biblical patriarch Abraham and the son Isaac who was once offered up as a sacrifice and we are reminded of Ikemefuma, who was in fact sacrificed and whose death Nwoye never forgave and Okonkwo never recovered from."[174] Okonkwo realises that the clan and most of his beloved have turned against him; as a result, he refuses the new order by killing himself.

IV.9. The Personal Destiny: "chi"

'Chi' is the belief in departed ancestors as the living dead with whom one can hold daily communion through various offerings and upon whom one can rely for health, wealth and protection; belief in the earth god as the ultimate judge of morality and good conduct; belief in oracles, in benevolent and malevolent spirits and gods; and belief in one Supreme being, 'Chukwu,' as the creator of the world. Another important feature are the oracles and shrines, which were used to make appeals to the gods. The Igbo people worshipped a variety of minor gods but the most important deities were 'Chukwu' who was responsible for fertility and creation, and 'Ala,' the earth goddess; moreover, everybody had his personal god or 'chi' and the important memory of the ancestors. The personal 'chi' seemed decisive for the individual fate because it "…is granted to everyone by Chukwu at the moment of conception, a soul or spiritual double, to whom his fortune and abilities are ascribed. The chi fulfils the destiny which the creator has determined and at the moment of reincarnation bargains with him on behalf of the individual for improved status in the next life."[175] Okonkwo dehumanises himself against all basic human feelings. "The climax of his degeneracy is seen in his act of cutting down Ikemefuma, the boy who had been like one of his sons. It is Okonkwo's act of hubris that destroys him; afraid of being thought weak, he oversteps his role in society and at the same time offends against the gods, his

---

[173] Ibid. 180.
[174] Lawrence, *Long Drums and Cannons* 104.
[175] David, *Chinua Achebe* 16.

chi."[176] Okonkwo was determined to a great extent not to end like his father, in humiliation and buried like a dog; therefore, he tried to fight against his chi or fate but had to yield in the end to the mightier force in his life. He was destined to die in humiliation and leave behind him a new generation that was still divided between old customs and new Christian rules. He was not chosen to outlive the Christian invasion as the episode with the gun shows: at the funeral of a clan member, Okonkwo is taking part in the wild outburst of emotion proper to the occasion – firing of guns, slashing of bushes, leaping, dancing and shouting. In the midst of all this his gun explodes and a piece of it kills the son of the dead man, who is standing beside him.

> He fails objectively to control his modern weapon. Thereby he shows himself unfit not only for true traditional responsibility but for the even heavier responsibility that further enlightenment and modern lethal instruments impose on men. The novel illustrates not only the gulf that can yawn between the African point of view and the white man's but also the hiatus that gaps between perennial standards of behaviour true and false.[177]

Kortenaar summarizes Okonkwo's life and death in a way that shows that he had had no choice but to end his opposition by a noble gesture:

> Okonkwo who hangs from the tree at the end is the son of the man who could not be properly buried, the warrior who must forever prove his own courage, the wealthy man who has taken the second highest title in the land, the short-tempered husband quick to suspect insubordination and to beat his wives, the wearer of a spirit mask, the father who is rejected in his turn by his own son, the man who wrestles with his chi, and the killer of the white man's messenger. He is alive and he is dead, and he could not be anywhere else than hanging on that tree.[178]

---

[176] Ernest N. Emenyonu, *The Rise of the Ibo Novel* (Oxford: Oxford UP, 1978) 119-22.

[177] *African-English Literature: A Short Survey and Anthology of Prose and Poetry up to 1965*, ed. Anne Tibble (London: Peter Owen, 1965) 104-6.

[178] Kortenaar, *Postcolonial Literatures: Achebe, Ngugi, Desai, Walcott* 48.

IV.10. The Missionaries and the District Commissioner's Descent

"The missionaries had come to Umuofia." (Achebe 103) The African as he emerges from the security of the tribal life, which is being destroyed, needs someone to depend upon. He finds such a person in the European who is rich, powerful and immune to the local forces of magic. "The desire for dependence corresponds exactly to the psychological need of the colonial European. Coming from an aggressive, competitive society and determined to succeed, he needs above all else reassurance. The subservience of a dependent is the easiest way of satisfying that need. The problems arise when either the dependability or the subservience breaks down."[179] The missionaries were the intermediaries between the two fronts but they tried to undermine the importance of the indigenous gods and deities by telling the Igbos that they "worshipped false gods, gods of wood and stone." (Achebe 104) Obviously, the white man did label those customs as incomprehensible and meaningless. But also the natives were suspicious of the one God of the white missionaries. "To the white man's doctrine that there is only one God who has the earth, the sky and all men, the people concluded that they must be mad."[180] The missionaries came to Umuofia and brought with them a government that would protect the followers of the religion. They convinced some of the villagers to leave their old religion behind them by showing them that they did not die only because they had built their church on evil ground. Okonkwo did not want to accept the white man's intrusion and wanted to kill those who "defecate on the floor…" but it was too late because "this was a woman clan." (Achebe 115) Okonkwo is the last great warrior who worships the bond of kinship but he is at the same time a tragic hero who does not realize that his situation is utterly hopeless and that his time and that of his clan has come. There is only one thing to do: to end this chapter of African history and glory, and the District Commissioner is the one who ends it. His ironic statement at the end of the novel proves the otherness of the Africans. The District Commissioner and the white man in general do not even make the attempt to understand or analyse the otherness they have encountered and that they are about to destroy. "What the District Commissioner finds of interest in Okonkwo's suicide is its mystery: its

---
[179] Carroll, *Chinua Achebe* 7.
[180] Julius N. Ogu, "The Concept of Madness in Chinua Achebe's Writings," *Journal of Commonwealth Literature* 18.1 (1983) 49.

impenetrability as an example of the foreignness, the difference of supposed primitives."[181] To stress the utter falsity of this version of events Achebe must re-establish the humanity of his Africans, must insist that Africans live in the same world and are not absolutely 'other.' Okonkwo's offer of military resistance to the white man, whom he correctly identifies with chaos, threatens to unleash the very chaos he hopes to keep at bay for the colonial regime needs just such an excuse to subject Umuofia to Abame's fate of extermination. "The white man is clever. He came quietly and peaceably with his religion. We were amused at his foolishness and allowed him to stay. Now he has won our brothers, and our clan can no longer act like one. He has put a knife on the things that held us together and we have fallen apart." (Achebe 127)

> The District Commissioner is an archetype of those numerous Europeans, particularly missionaries and administrators, whose instant expertise on Africa has contributed to the Westerner's profound ignorance of the continent. And the ethnocentric bias of the District Commissioner's imperial handbook underlines the historical inability of the Western scholar to emancipate himself from the usual perspectives on African 'primitives.'"[182]

He embodies the ignorant European colonizer who seeks to bring light to the darkness of a continent which is already illuminated by their own culture and thinking. But again, the supposed superiority of the white man is forced upon the Africans; moreover, men like him just waited for natives like Okonkwo to have a reason to wipe out people on a daily basis if they did not want to conform. As the narrative shows, there can be more benevolent characters among the whites such as the one before Rev. Smith who tried to communicate with the natives on a human basis; but violence seems to solve the problem properly and faster. The episode with the unmasked 'egwugwu' is the first step in that direction because it was considered to be a fatal crime. Enoch's act of violence leads to the destruction of the church on behalf of the Umuofians, but they are arrested and humiliated. That is the moment when Okonkwo knows what to do with his enemy, the District Commissioner and the white man in general: to fight for his existence even if he would have to do it alone. "But if they chose to be cowards he would go out and avenge himself." (Achebe 143) Both Okonkwo and the Commissioner are ignorant of the existence of the 'other.'

---

[181] Kortenaar, *Postcolonial Literatures: Achebe, Ngugi, Desai, Walcott* 32.
[182] Brown, *Critical Perspectives on Nigerian Literatures* 138.

Okonkwo lives in the past and the "District Commissioner is a typical Crusoe blind to the possibility that Friday could be a complex being with a complex culture. *Things Fall Apart* is Achebe's answer to years of Christian bigotry and Crusoe's naïve view of Friday."[183] Carroll David goes on to describe the Commissioner's point of view, "Africa is a world of primitive customs, heart of darkness of the European imagination. The shift of perspective from the inside to the outside of the fictional world is a device whose function is clear. It reminds us that the assumption we have come to accept in the course of the novel are not the only ones in that realm of experience we have been exploring."[184]

Africa with all its beauty and power is crumbling under the simultaneous pressures of white imperialism from without, and self-destructing forces from within. "The deliberate emphasis on black and white as the familiar cornerstones of white religion demonstrates that the maledictive patterns of the English language are integrated with the European's racial bias and cultural perceptions."[185] Rev. Smith conforms with the perceptual values which the French scholar Mannoni has ascribed to the colonial traditions embodied by the Prospero-Caliban myth: "What the colonial lack in common with Prospero, is awareness of the world of others, a world in which others have to be respected."[186] The threatening disintegration of the old traditions can be put down to the egocentric quality in African character as well as to the Europeans' exclusivism. "Okonkwo's egocentric failure to recognize or respect the humanity of Ikemefuma and Nwoye, is symptomatic of these weaknesses which have made his society vulnerable to the promises of Christianity."[187] Okonkwo lost his son to the Christians because Nwoye was captivated by the new religion, which did not kill his best friend or cast twins to the Evil Forest to let them die there. He was fascinated by the hymn of the Christian religion and could not cope with his origins anymore; therefore, he sought for salvation and found it in the white missionaries who could solve "the question of the twins crying in the bush and the question of Ikemefuma who was killed." (Achebe 106) Obierika thought about Okonkwo's destiny and that of his own twins as well; Nwoye and Obierika were the first ones to doubt and put into

---

[183] Ngugi Wa Thiong'o, *Homecoming: Essays on African and Caribbean Literature, Culture and Politics* (London: Heinemann, 1972) 51.
[184] Carroll, *Chinua Achebe* 60.
[185] Brown, *Critical Perspectives on Nigerian Literatures* 140.
[186] Dominique O. Mannoni, *Prospero and Caliban: The Psychology of Colonization*, trans. Pamela Powesland (London: Heinemann, 1956) 108.
[187] Brown, *Critical Perspectives on Nigerian Literatures* 142.

question the way of life of Igbo society. Nwoye is the one who found the courage to stand up against his father and the whole tribe to join the Christians. Okonkwo saw in Nwoye the ultimate germ of destruction for the whole clan. Moreover, he was faced with the destiny of his own father and concluded "If such a thing were ever to happen, he, Okonkwo, would wipe them off the face of the earth." (Achebe 110) He killed the messenger when he tried to stop the meeting. Okonkwo immediately realized that he was on a lonely path where nobody had followed him. He killed himself and could not be taken down by his fellow villagers because "it is an abomination for a man to take his own life…" the greatest man in Umuofia was dead and "…he will be buried like a dog." (Achebe 149) His death seems not to be important for the further development of the Christian mission in Africa, and therefore, the Commissioner reduces Okonkwo's life to a chapter of the book he intends to write. "Perhaps not a whole chapter but a reasonable paragraph, at any rate. There was much else to include, and one must be firm in cutting out details. He had already chosen the title of the book, after much thought: *The Pacification of the Primitive Tribes of the Lower Niger*." (Achebe 150) Okonkwo's life and that of the Igbo people is reduced to a detail in the process of civilizing the 'African barbarians.' The mission is accomplished and all the details on the way to the succession are of no importance. This is the ultimate proof for the ignorance of the white missionaries in tackling with cultures other than their own.

V. *Abyssinian Chronicles*
V.1. The Life and Works of Moses Isegawa

Moses Isegawa was born in Kampala, Uganda, in 1963. He received his education in a seminary, and then worked as a history teacher for four years. In 1990, he left Uganda for the Netherlands and is now a Dutch citizen. *Abyssinian Chronicles* is his first novel.

V.2. Introduction to *Abyssinian Chronicles*

The teller of this panoramic tale is Mugezi, a quick-witted and sharp-eyed man whose life encompasses the traditional and the modern, the peaceful and the insanely violent, the despotic and the democratic. Born in a rural community in early 1960, he is raised by his grandfather, a deposed clan chief, and his grandaunt, or 'grandmother,' after his parents immigrate to the capital city of Kampala. At the age of nine, he leaves behind his secure life in the village to join his parents and siblings in the city, where he is first exposed to the despotism and hardship that he will contend with in the years to come.

The nightmare reign of Idi Amin and its chaotic aftermath are the backdrop to Mugezi's troubled coming-of-age: his constant struggle with his harsh mother and austere father; his years spent as caregiver to his parents' ever-growing brood of children; his sojourn in a horrifically repressive Catholic seminary. He goes on to work as a high school teacher, becomes enmeshed in a tragic romance, finds himself drawn into a dubious, potentially dangerous alliance with the military after Amin's fall and witnesses the wide-spread ravages of the AIDS virus. Finally, sickened by personal loss and national tragedy, he manages to immigrate to Amsterdam.

"It is a great irony of history and geography," wrote Chinua Achebe, "that Africa, whose land mass is closer than any other to the mainland of Europe, should come to occupy in European psychological disposition the farthest point of otherness, should indeed become Europe's very antithesis."[188] The title *Abyssinian Chronicles* is not a geographical or historical mistake and it has nothing to do with ancient Ethiopia. The first question to be asked is why the title of the book is not *Ugandan Chronicles* since it is obviously about Uganda. The explanation for the title comes very late in the novel when the narrator says it is the only political statement his father ever made:

> He said that Uganda was a land of false bottoms where under every abyss there was another one waiting to snare people, and that the historians had made a mistake: Abyssinia was not the ancient land of Ethiopia, but modern Uganda...for he believed that the time had come to change the name Uganda to Abyssinia.[189]

"Mugezi and all the members of his extended family play out, in microcosm, the upheavals of post-colonial Africa: the diaspora from stable rural societies into hectic cities governed by money rather than loyalties."[190] Moses Isegawa's large novel is clearly based on the author's own life. His first person narrator, Mugezi, is about the same age, suffers the same schooling, becomes a teacher, and finally leaves his native Uganda for the Netherlands, making a new life there. The story describes the battles of 1950, as Protestantism and Catholicism vie with the Islam and traditional beliefs. Christianity proves a target, notably in Mugezi's parents. Nevertheless, Islam and the other religions seem to play a big role throughout the book as Isegawa introduces Catholic, Protestant, and Muslim characters, and does a fine job of describing their missionary approaches and zeal. Uganda was and is a complex place of many different ethnic and religious groupings.

---

[188] Maya Jaggi, "Into the Heart of Grunge," *The Guardian* November 18 (2000), 2 February 2001 <http://www.booksunlimited.co.uk/reviews/generalfiction/0,6121,399107,00.htm>.

[189] Moses Isegawa, *Abyssinian Chronicles* (New York: Alfred A. Knopf, 2000) 440. Further references to the book will be made with parenthetical documentation.

[190] Paul Gray, "Coming of Age in Chaos," *Time Europe* 156 May (2000), 2 February 2001 <http://www.time.com/time/europe/magazine/2000/0731/gray.htm>.

V.3. The History of Uganda in the Second Half of the 20th Century

In 1962 Uganda gained independence from British rule[191] and in 1963 Kabaka Mutesa II became president. A year later African troops mutinied at Jinja and British troops were called in. In April 1964, within months of the mutiny, the General Service Unit (GSU) was set up by the government as a paramilitary force under the control of Akena Adoko, a close associate of Prime Minister Milton Obote. After the mutiny Israel soon became Uganda's main military supplier. Under the new government Colonel Idi Amin was promoted several times and achieved the second highest ranking in the Army. During the absence of Obote, the Parliament called for the suspension of Colonel Amin, the Deputy Commander of the Ugandan Army, while an investigation of his bank account was undertaken. However, he was not suspended as Parliament had resolved, for that would have had wide-reaching implications. In 1966 Milton Obote suspended the constitution of 1962, introduced an interim constitution and proclaimed himself Executive President. Obote tried to secure his political supremacy and unite the country under his leadership; that meant to eliminate from key positions supporters and associates of those who had lost out in the power struggle of 1966, to treat the Army with favour, in an attempt to bring it under his control, and to de-emphasise his reliance on the army by moving to the Left. In the course of this shift a rupture developed between Obote and the Commander of the Army, Major-General Idi Amin. In 1970 Obote stripped Amin of most of his powers and appointed Brigadier Hussein and Colonel Musa to assume responsibility for running the Army.

In order to resolve the conflict between himself and the President, Amin staged a take-over of government by the military in a coup on 25 February 1971. Amin was not considered to have any political ambitions himself, and therefore must have acted for personal reasons. Powerless to rally his supporters and put down the coup, Obote spent the next ten years in Tanzania as a political refugee. *The Financial Times* voted Amin 'Man of the Week'; little consideration was given to the possible consequences of the coup for the Ugandan populace as a whole. Amin made an early promise to hold fair and free elections. Soon the soldiers under his command were divided and

---

[191] the following information about the historical situation of Uganda is taken from Amii Omava-Otunnu, *Politics and the Military in Uganda, 1890-1985* (London: Macmillan, 1987) 65-169.

undisciplined, and they took advantage of the situation to engage in indiscriminate harassment of the civilian population for their own ends. He promoted himself President, and the people realised that there would not be any free elections during his regime. His next step was to set off to visit countries which had played a role in aiding him to power and promoting his regime. Amin unilaterally terminated diplomatic relations with Israel and turned to Libya for support since Qadhafi had suggested that the conflicts in the Middle East stemmed from an opposition between Judaism and Islam, and that it was therefore Amin's responsibility to take the side of Islam. On August 24 1972, he ordered all Asians holding British passports and nationals of India, Pakistan and Bangladesh to leave the country. Although as part of his strategy for survival Amin terrorised the civil population and put fear into his troops, he also tried to keep the soldiers contented by offering them scope for looting and for taking bribes. Within the country the population had become increasingly disenchanted with the regime because of the terror and the shortages of the essential commodities such as sugar, salt, matches, cooking oil and bread.

The murder of Archbishop Luwum marked the beginning of Amin's prosecution of Christians in 1977. On April 11, 1979 Kampala was liberated from Amin's hold and the country was effectively rid of him; he left behind him a legacy of colossal destruction as his regime was primarily based on violence. The new administration was confronted with a monumental task of reconstruction and rehabilitation, which called for dedication and sacrifice. Milton Obote came once again to power but was overthrown not long after, in 1985. The hopes, which had been aroused by the return of an elected civilian government after the 1980 victory of Obote and the UPC, were endangered from the start by the rival claimants to political power who had been disappointed by the election results. The guerrilla warfare that ensued was fought essentially along ethnic lines. The apparent strength of the guerrilla forces was not because they were numerically or militarily strong within the country, but because they managed to get substantial aid from international sources. As already mentioned, the second coup took place in 1985, its most disruptive effect being the looting which erupted in Kampala in the days immediately afterwards. On 17 December 1985, a peace accord was signed in Nairobi.

V.4. Isegawa's Style and Language

The book starts with the description of the death of Mugezi's father, Serenity, and we immediately feel the presence of an omniscient narrator within the story. "Any novel that begins with a man on the brink of being eaten by a crocodile stands a god chance of engaging a reader's attention."[192] The narrator presents the story from different perspectives as he recounts the various fates of the main protagonists. He starts with Serenity and Padlock, Mugezi's parents, then goes on with his relatives but he basically relies on Mugezi's fate intertwined with the history of Uganda in the second half of the 20th century. As it has been mentioned before, the book bears resemblance to elements of the so-called 'magic realism' because primarily the beginning and the end are characterised by fantastic elements such as the death of Mugezi's parents because she is killed by a bull and he is eaten by a crocodile. Based on the military background of Idi Amin's regime and its aftermath, Moses Isegawa tries to find a new way of defining his identity and that of the black continent. Once again the creation of a modern and challenging language seems to be the key to the redefinition of new modes of thinking for the decolonised Africans in general. Isegawa's style is modern, rough and sometimes even shocking because it applies violence to tear down the old barricades and structures for the identity quest. Isegawa depicts the life of his family in the country immediately after independence and shortly before Amin's rise to power. The figure of the grandmother represents security and balance and is in contrast to the 'lively' or rather dreadful life in the city. The female dimension helps the author to try to define his style and language throughout the book; it is the lack of the female element in the main protagonists Serenity and Mugezi that makes their quest a struggle for freedom. Quite contrarily, Padlock is portrayed as a religious 'beast' that tries to acknowledge the realities and brutalities of Uganda through her religious belief, which proves so strong that she cannot even distinguish between reality and illusion.

Through the use of his 'english' Moses Isegawa creates a language with new tendencies. The mixture of different elements, on the one hand, enables him to recreate the atmosphere of Kampala before the coup, and on the other, the atrocities

---

[192] Jim Price, "Isegawa Chronicles Pain, Passions of Central Africa," *Milwaukee Journal Sentinel* June 16 (2000)
<http://www.jsonline.com/entbooks/reviews/jun00/bk.abyss18061600as.htm>.

and the destruction of ideals during and in particular after 1977. Untranslated words such as *muteego*, AIDS, *matooke*, plantain, and *posho*, corn bread, and code switching such as "Osiibye otya nnyabo?" (Isegawa 422) highlight the indigenous character of the book about Uganda together with the lack of self-confidence and orientation during the period of decolonisation. The return to the metropolis, the centre of racism, imperialism and capitalism marks the creation of a new language, a new 'english,' on which the author Moses Isegawa relies in order not to blow up his mind and being spewed, but to seek the code to be able to go on a quest for a new identity.

V.5. Post-Independent Search of Identity
V.5.1. Woman and Religion

In the first chapter Isegawa's narrator, Mugezi, whom Christina Patterson compares with Tristram Shandy,[193] describes the childhood of his father as the son of the local clan chief and a mother who ran off with a shopkeeper. This resulted in a deep aversion to the Indian shopkeepers because they had taken away his mother and at the same time part of his identity; furthermore, they represented the imperialistic presence on the African continent, especially in Uganda. Serenity "saw those Indians and those few Africans who owned shops, and the faceless financiers and manufacturers, as a species of silver-tongued man-eaters ready to tear people to bits". (Isegawa 27) He was never able to deal with the fact that his mother had left him for "…sacks of sugar, salt and beans, packets of sweets, matches and exercise books…" which "made him shrivel with insignificance" and at the same time "exuded an air of preciousness, desirability and indispensability so profound that he could not bear to look at the way they were cared for and secured." (Isegawa 27)

Serenity had lost his faith in women until in a fit of independence he made an extremely unwise choice in proposing to Nakkazi, also known as Virgin, St. Peter, or finally Padlock. She had been a nun and was caught beating children so badly "that she was disrobed and thrust back into a world she was both ill-suited for and did not

---

[193] Christina Patterson, "Amin was his Saviour. Until Reality Set In," *The Guardian* November 12 (2000) <http://www.booksunlimited.co.uk/Print/0,3858,4089735,00.htm>.

like. Marriage was a perverse martyrdom for her and she made as many others suffer for it as she could."[194] The figure of Padlock is portrayed as being very religious, and therefore, the narrator has uses many metaphors to describe her character and her outstanding marriage with Serenity. Mugezi's father pinned down Padlock's character as the three heads of the "hydra":

> The first head breathed the harsh poison of ultraconservative Catholicism: the type which stifled personal enterprise, glorified poverty and hard labour, extolled stoicism, execrated politics and focused on heaven. The second head spewed dictatorship: the all-authority-is-from-God type and obedience without question. The third head was responsible for violent temper, Virgin being a second-generation sufferer, and the defence of indefensible contradictory positions, like the church's stand on abortion, contraception and celibacy. (Isegawa 28)

Virgin prayed "nine consecutive novenas to St. Jude Thaddeus" (Isegawa 36) in order to be sure that Serenity was the right man for her because "such an individual had to undergo some mortification to achieve the purification necessary to enter into holy matrimony with a virgin." (Isegawa 36) The account of the wedding of Mugezi's parents is extremely gripping because of "its sharp sexual edge, its lewd undertones, its aggressive joy" (Isegawa 37), Padlock's prudish horror at the offensive gyrations of the dancers. Virgin had the impression that "the crowd was fucking her, raping her, deflowering her, gobbling the rivers of blood that poured from her cavities...she visualized Jesus on the cross, all blood, all wounds, all pain." (Isegawa 39) We get the impression of a virgin who suffers for all the human beings on earth; moreover, she is a woman who sacrifices herself in order to rescue people, especially her husband and the whole family, from damnation. Further on, in the wedding night, when Serenity found that erections "seemed to be manufactured in a factory far away," (Isegawa 40) we are prepared for his futile first sex with his new wife. It is baled out by the helpful intervention of a bridal aunt who subsequently became his mistress. In the end we are left with the rivers of vomit and diarrhoea flooding the village after the wedding feast. Virgin, now Padlock, saw it as her duty to free the people around her from the devil because they were all doomed to die without witnessing the holy communion with God. She hated Serenity's family and therefore projected all her hate on Mugezi.

---

[194] "Abyssinian Chronicles," *The Borzoi Reader* Summer (2000)
<http://www.randomhouse.com/knopf/borzoi/2000summer/isegawa.htm>.

When Serenity got a job in Kampala, he and Padlock moved there while Mugezi spent the first years in the baby business with his great-aunt "as a midwife's mascot-cum-assistant." (Isegawa 67) The 1966 state of emergency had passed without inflicting much damage on the area of Mpande Hill. On January 25, 1971 his world came crashing down: the night Idi Amin took power was also the night his grandmother died.

> General Idi Amin, helped by his British and Israeli friends, seized power in a military coup. He overthrew his former benefactor, Milton Obote, the prime minister who had led the country to independence and had gone on to suspend the constitution. General Amin gave eighteen reasons for the coup, among them corruption, detention without trial, lack of freedom of speech and economic mismanagement of the country. (Isegawa 81)

These listed reasons promised a better future for the Ugandan population. As history has shown, all his promises proofed lies as he reigned the country even more brutally than it had been done before. After his grandmother had died, Mugezi moved to the city of Kampala to join his parents with their brood of children. His mother's nickname appears to have switched from Virgin to Padlock making him do all the dirty work, allowing him almost no respite. According to Patterson "Mugezi's excremental duties are an apt metaphor for the punishing regime in which he finds himself trapped. Padlock proves more power-crazed than any dictator, forcing Mugezi to kneel before her for hours on end and rewarding every minor and imagined misdemeanour with savage thrashings."[195] Padlock changes and becomes more self-confident after she reinforced the rules in her house. She embodies the figure of the dictator who brutally denigrates and rules over her people. In addition, she can be compared to Idi Amin, who operated on a national scale, while she terrorized Mugezi on the domestic level; he hates his mother but he admires the General, even if only during the first period of his reign. Serenity can be seen as a silent collaborator because he does not have any power in the familial hierarchy because he is mesmerized by another world with different rules, a world created by Dickens and *Waiting for Godot*. "He loved operating in a web of unuttered threats, restrained violence and low-voiced warnings...He let it be known, indirectly, that he never interfered with the work of his enforcer, except in the most dire of circumstances." (Isegawa 95-96) He lost part of his identity because of his mother's

---

[195] Patterson, <http://www.booksunlimited.co.uk/Print/0,3858,4089735,00.htm>.

lack of courage that resulted in her leaving. His identity is further spoilt when he marries Padlock who strongly believes in God, and therefore epitomizes his antithesis. Serenity is desperately looking for something outside himself because he does not believe in himself; that is perhaps the reason why he dedicates his leisure time to the reading of *Waiting for Godot*. He is waiting and pretending to be able to explain the world amid his rational behaviour and premises. He does not realise that God is already inside him from the beginning, and that is why he keeps looking for the divine existence outside his own being. "He was hiding and waiting for the arrival of Godot. He forgot that I had usurped the role of Godot. Serenity tends to like authors-like Beckett and Dickens-who had had difficulties with their mothers." (Isegawa 135) The figure of the woman seems to be an especially important feature throughout the book since the story is based on the relationship of the male protagonists towards their mothers, wives and lovers. Serenity, as well as Mugezi, tries to find his lost identity because the loss of the mother figure obviously caused a lack of identity. Serenity lost his mother and therefore, cannot cope with the newly created situation of a married man. As a result, he is alienated from any woman and especially from his wife who proves to be extremely religious. As a matter of fact she succeeds in destroying him, and that is why he becomes involved with her aunt. Mugezi, alternatively, considers his 'grandmother' to be his 'real' mother, not Padlock. As the story illustrates, he has problems in dealing with women as well and as a result, his efforts to find his identity are reflected in the women of the story. Furthermore, British colonialism, Idi Amin's perverse regime, and the chaotic aftermath destroyed his notion of identity he has been looking for since he is a boy. On August 24, 1972 Mugezi's childhood fantasy comes true when Amin expels all the nation's shopkeepers, indeed all Indians, and everybody seems delighted that these agents of British colonial oppression have been forced out. While Mugezi tries to live through his mother's dictatorship, he observes Idi Amin's regime with growing admiration although he never succumbs to the man's charms. Mugezi suffers a great deal, "not because he is naturally a victim but because he lives in a thoroughly unjust and arbitrary world. His domestic and school life mirror, on a different scale, the life of most Ugandans under the perverse regime of Idi Amin."[196] Mugezi returns to the recollection of his grandfather who experienced the suspension of the constitution in 1966. He lived through his own downfall and that of his country at the same time:

---

[196] "Complete Review," <http://www.complete-review.com/reviews/uganda/isegawa.htm>.

> Armed soldiers were stationed in Grandpa's village for the first time in national history. He believed that the time had come for the national edifice to go up in flames. He stoked the conflagration with the oil of his eloquence. He spoke to the political idiots about their no-win situation in biting parables. He acted with the bravery of a man who knew that destiny was on his side. (Isegawa 117)

He expected Milton Obote to "lead the country down the red road of Communism or Socialism...to see the nationalization of Indian businesses, and British military intervention to protect the interests of British capital." (Isegawa 117) But nothing happens because Idi Amin takes control of the country on the national level; on the familial level he takes away Mugezi's 'grandmother.' Mugezi learns to deal with the harsh conditions created by his own father and mother at home, developing into a 'domestic guerrilla.' "Thus, Mugezi trades a small-time, petty despotism for a much larger one, and in the role of soldier-bureaucrats he learns how merciless life can really be."[197] The situation gets out of control when he is beaten into submission by Padlock, and as a result, Serenity withdraws into his own world trying to hide from reality and transcend into the world of ideals. The role of Padlock is particularly decisive for the development of the story since she embodies Catholicism: "the nun in her never died." (Isegawa 159) She is uncomfortable with her aunt Nakibuka because she saw her naked and touched her husband in the night of their first sex; she helped him to get an erection. "In those days, one never looked at oneself, even if one bathed or pulled devil hair. The body belonged to Christ, and to Christ alone." (Isegawa 159) Isegawa goes on to describe her religious obsession, as "Nunhood, the convent and the vows, were things that would speak to her for the rest of her life. Nunhood, she said to the walls, makes a woman a woman among women, a priestess, a goddess, a queen of heaven." (Isegawa 163) This obsession goes hand in hand with her being the representative of colonialism because she sees nothing wrong in the procedure of colonizing non-white people. She considers the Israelis and the whites to be blessed by the "book":

> In her mind, the white races could do no wrong as long as they fulfilled what God commissioned them to do: to go out, conquer the world and save it from the threat of Islam. All the darker races had to do was to accept the deal, offering their labour and resources in

---

[197] Price, <http://www.jsonline.com/entbooks/reviews/jun00/bk.abyss18061600as.htm>.

return. For that reason, she saw nothing wrong with the old missionary tactics of sugar-coated invasion, fomentation of religious wars and political interference. (Isegawa 174)

At the end of chapter three, Mugezi reflects on the vital question of British colonialism:

>...by and by I asked myself the right questions: Did Cane mean that if our chiefs had not been divided-Protestants, Catholics, Muslims, pagans-they would have stopped the spread of British colonial rule and imperialism? Did we, at the turn of the century, have military superiority over British forces in the East African region?...No, Cane was wrong: the British would have come anyway. (Isegawa 179)

Religious differences among the to-be-conquered are basically an essential factor for the success of the Europeans and their 'mission.' Mugezi and all the others in the story seek to analyse their identity. Imperialism imposed its rules and convictions on the conquered people, robbed them of their identity and culture, only to leave them wondering about their position in the world. When he finally leaves for Amsterdam, he believes to escape racism but ends up in exactly the same environment as before: under the pressure of colonial presence.

V.6. White Religion as a Futile Attempt to Lessen Colonial Impact

Mugezi is sent to a Catholic seminary, a place of even more unspeakable and arbitrary terror, both from other students and teachers. The chapter describes Mugezi's sojourn at the seminary and his attempts to survive the harsh environment created by the teachers and fellow students. On the one hand he tries to impress the teachers who are dear to him, and on the other hand he succeeds in driving others out of the seminary. Particularly the arrival of Fr.Gilles Lageau, a French Canadian missionary from Quebec, makes Mugezi apprehend the circumstances of the era he is living in. "The era of the white missionaries had ended. They started the Church in Uganda almost one hundred years ago." (Isegawa 215) As time went by, more and more indigenous archbishops, cardinals, and bishops "manned the Catholic Church."

(Isegawa 215) There was a fear that one day the work of the white missionaries would be taken over by the black people, "because most of the work done now was in Africa and vocations in Europe were almost gone." (Isegawa 215) Lageau's presence seemed to prove this as his zeal was believed to be the revolution of the seminary. Mugezi is "mesmerised by the power machinations of a rich, white European priest and adept at making his own Machiavellian manoeuvres in order to prosper and survive."[198]

Mugezi interrupts his account of the seminary to throw in the Holy Year and the Pilgrimage to Israel and Rome in 1975 when Serenity and Padlock witness the greatest event in the history of their lives. "Serenity felt a bit like Jesus…He wanted to be somebody to outlast time, a Jesus-like ghost who would sprinkle his name on the sands of time, a free spirit who would inspire strangers with the universal seed embedded in its home-grown fruit." (Isegawa 237) The trip to Israel is Padlock's ultimate fulfilment of her most secret dreams because she leaves behind her past and wants to carry on making people discover the might of Christ and Catholicism. "She was the virgin raised from the mud and the bush of a lowly village to the triumph of birthing God's son and bringing salvation to all. She was the virgin of Nazareth…" (Isegawa 240) She is completely absorbed by the atmosphere of the holy place and swears to herself to bring salvation to all the damned souls out there, especially her family. Once again, the Roman Catholic religion plays a significant role in trying to come to terms with the problems of imperialism and the loss of identity. Padlock seeks answers and she finds them in her deeply rooted religious faith, but for Mugezi religion is not to help him find his answers.

When Mugezi finally damages Lageau's holy boat called *Agatha*, he destroys his dearest possession. "Why did it have to be sacred *Agatha*? Who did not know that Agatha happened to be the name of his mother, his first girlfriend and his ideal woman? Who did not know that *Agatha* brought out all the protective instincts in him?" (Isegawa 247) Once again, religion takes on a very crucial role because Lageau came to the seminary to talk about the benefits of Jesus and his holy deeds, and indeed "Lageau reminded me of Jesus cursing the Pharisees, …yes, this man was the reincarnation of Jesus." (Isegawa 249) He compares Lageau to Padlock and asks himself whether that man did something special in his life. "As Padlock had not created the uterus, Lageau had not invented money-or knowledge or power, for that

---

[198] Patterson, <http://www.booksunlimited.co.uk/Print/0,3858,4089735,00.htm>.

matter." (Isegawa 251) He had not invented something new because "he was merely regurgitating hundreds of years of philosophical, social and political vomit." (Isegawa 251) In attacking Lageau, Mugezi assails at the same time the Catholic Church together with its faith, because Lageau as a representative embodies his forebears, "the agents of the holy armadillo who had waged wars and poisoned our politics with religion. Hadn't General Amin, time and again, charged that the Catholic Church was built on murder, terror, senseless war, genocide and robbery?" (Isegawa 252) Mugezi goes on with a biting condemnation of the church and its representatives throughout history

> Apart from their colour, what had they added to priesthood? Had they expanded the vision of life and spirituality? Had they combated suffering or added to human knowledge in any special way? When they opened their mouths, they merely regurgitated rotting Church rules, worm-infested dogmas and slimy platitudes created in the burrows of the holy armadillo. They were just perpetuating the stink-old order: white, nuclear-warhead-privileged priests above the black, shit-scared peasant priest, who was above the shitty-assed peasant nun, who lorded it over the wormy peasant faithful-man, woman, child. Hundreds of years of Catholic dictatorship later, ninety-five of them home-grown, had come only to this! What a waste! (Isegawa 253)

The importance of such a statement in which he condemns colonialism and imperialism is apparent. He asks himself whether those centuries of white dictatorship had caused any positive results, but all he can conclude is that it had been a futile attempt. The dehumanisation of the 'other' races had resulted in destruction, loss of identity, violence and damage, which would prevent people from coping with their past for a long time.

V.7. Amin's Heritage

In 1979 Uganda was liberated from Amin's brutal regime and consequently, acts of brutality occurred on all levels. Among the worst was the torture of Lwandeka, Padlock's younger sister, by guerrillas and the rape of Kasawo, Padlock's other sister, by troops that helped to depose Amin, and who otherwise did little harm to the local population. "Uganda was in a state of siege, writhing like a dying moth on the floor." (Isegawa 286) Uganda was surrounded by those who wanted to depose Amin and free the country from his firm grip. Among them "General Amin's predecessor, Milton Obote, and anti-Amin guerrillas who were gathering, whipping themselves into attacking form and making brave incursions into Uganda. Using Radio Tanzania, their leaders called upon the Ugandans to get rid of Amin." (Isegawa 286)

By the time Mugezi leaves the seminary, the country was almost completely corrupted. He cannot get a place at the university to study law, his grandfather's dream for him. Getting a place now depends on contacts, bribes, connections, and luck, and even resourceful Mugezi cannot navigate this particular maze. He becomes a teacher and the pay is so low that no teacher could live on that salary alone. After leaving the seminary, his ideas and opinions develop. Initially he was attracted by Amin's regime but then "my flirtation with General Amin had ended, killed by the murderous light of truth." (Isegawa 266) Patterson beautifully describes the situation by reporting that "as Uganda lurched into the horrific aftermath of the Amin regime, he realised that he had 'dammed his disgust' with the reality of the political situation 'just to keep fighting in my corner.'"[199] Mugezi describes "Amin as a ghostly spectre who had come to destabilize and pollute the nation by accentuating the evil within. My uninformed view was that the seeds sown were going to germinate, and that the worst was yet to come." (Isegawa 297) The readers are witnesses of the horrible status quo after the coup in 1979. Furthermore, Mugezi's village had been attacked and reduced to a scene of destruction; during the attack his grandfather was killed by the guerrillas. He had lived through Uganda's history, and was therefore "an encyclopaedia of our political history." (Isegawa 313) Mugezi recalls the wreckages of the coup and the importance of Tanzania, which played a decisive role in restructuring the country. "It was evident that getting rid of a tyrant was one thing,

---

[199] Patterson, <http://www.booksunlimited.co.uk/Print/0,3858,4089735,00.htm>.

setting the house in order quite another." (Isegawa 318) Padlock once again tries to convert her sister Kasawo by telling her "God sent Amin's henchmen to wake her up from the complacency of sin" because "you pissed down God's throat too and wiped your bottom on His plans for you." (Isegawa 327) Padlock is of the opinion that Amin was God's chastisement for the people of Uganda and especially for people like her sister; the white man sinned against God and was punished. "God cut the white man with his own sword...he turned the white man's black collaborators into his worst enemies." (Isegawa 327) Then it was the turn of the Indians who were punished for their greed, and the black man rejoiced. "But instead of learning a lesson and turning to God, the black man took everything for granted." (Isegawa 328); this is why he was punished through Amin and his regime.

At the end of chapter five, Mugezi is attacked and raped by a group of women. He explains it as "the only pattern I could discern was that I had become another statistic in our family history. I too had been violated, and my tormentors had escaped unscathed." (Isegawa 340) Mugezi becomes a symbol for his country because he suffered from the attacks of his mother, a dictator on the familial scale. Shortly after Amin was deposed, he experiences the brutal atmosphere of Amin's aftermath. "Guerrilla war broke out." (Isegawa 340) The "mathematical configuration of death, the Luwero Triangle, which had first appeared in 1978, returned to haunt us...The uncanny quality of this triangle was that it contracted and expanded at will as guerrillas moved from place to place attacking or fleeing government forces." (Isegawa 344) The guerrillas set up a provisional government and cut the country in two. The government and the guerrillas agree on a cease-fire but then accuse each other of violating it. "Finally, the agreement between the guerrillas and the government was signed. Within a matter of weeks, however, the fighting picked up steam, and the guerrillas captured Kampala on January 25, 1986." (Isegawa 362) Mugezi, then a corrupt anti-corruption agent, finds his village overrun by coffee-smuggling youths in bell-bottoms, platform shoes and Afro-wigs. At the same time the expelled Indians return under IMF fiat, and Mugezi observes that "I was becoming convinced that the afterbirth of war was in ways worse than the actual fighting itself, and that winning the peace was harder than winning the war." (Isegawa 377)

Mugezi was able to supplement his income with a booming home brewery business until the brewery burns down and leaves him with nothing. The guerrilla war continues, and finally there is an attack on his home village, which results in destroying it.

> Oh, it made the actual shooting pale in significance. Here you were, waiting, fearing, and then the moment comes. It is a sort of anti-climax, and you want it repeated: the terrible fear, the loin fire, the climactic anti-climatic shooting, the target falling. Punching is more satisfactory, physically speaking. The thing I remember most is the gun smoke and the explosions. (Isegawa 395)

Mugezi realizes that he has to carry on and forget his village because "...I felt disconnected, floating like a piece of wood on a lake. I knew that this was my last time here. So many ruins, so little life...It was time to leave." (Isegawa 408) At the same time Aids or 'Slim' spreads over the country and claims many deaths, among them Mugezi's aunt Lwandeka. After a series of affairs, most illicit, among them his own half-sister, and after being a teacher and not being able to afford living on his income, he flees the country in the hope of finding a more human environment. In fact, he starts a whole new life as a black man in the land of the colonizers and is once again the target of prejudice and racism.

V.8. Back to the Imperial Metropolis

In the final chapter the story shifts to Amsterdam, as Mugezi is sent to "a Dutch aid organization called Action II which had landed in trouble over child pornography." (Isegawa 414) He should speak to the Ugandan aid workers and in return he should fund-raise for them, getting free accommodation and food. Maya Jaggi worthily points our attention to a common theme by stating "he directs his vengeful and war-scarred vision at a European heart of darkness,"[200] as he is scared and disgusted by

> indifference of the wealthy West...They not only targeted geriatrics, but also spread the shrapnel over a wild field, hitting the constituency they believed had to be rubbed with shit and flies before releasing a dollar here, a dime there. The caustic magnesium burst of

---

[200] Jaggi, <http://www.booksunlimited.co.uk/reviews/generalfiction/0,6121,399107,00.htm>.

> Reaganomics and Thatcherite liberalism had penetrated deep into the aid cartels and empires, and finding myself in its residual glare did my eyes and my sensibilities no good. (Isegawa 420)

'A European heart of darkness,' anew I am assured that it is not Africa, but basically Europe which stands for the 'heart of darkness.' Mugezi leaves his native country only to embark on a more difficult mission, which leads him to the centre of racism, violence and power. He does not realise the danger of his sojourn to the Netherlands as it represents the source of his lost identity because Europe embodies imperialism. But obviously this is the right track because he traces down his enemy, and in facing his worst fears, he strives to rebuild a new identity based on the ruins of his national and domestic war. It is the white man who brought destruction to the black continent and wondered about the 'heart of darkness.' Nevertheless, it is the white Europe that was dark, or even pitch black and empirically racist, and to a certain extent it is still today.

Reborn with a false British passport, Mugezi tries to establish his own life and past. "The humanity in the depiction of Mugezi's aunt's death from Aids, and the sympathy for African women are replaced by a cold misogyny towards Amsterdam prostitutes, and a perfunctory effort to humanise Indian shopkeepers."[201] In Amsterdam he gets involved in love affairs with his landlady Eva and another girl named Magdelein. As a result, he realizes that he is not going to sacrifice his sanity for a white woman because he faces another personal tyranny of sex and racism to escape. His landlady Eva is another dictator in the form of a woman who cannot enrich Mugezi's horizon; she is the personification of the white colonizer who looks down on the 'other.' She is superficial, possessive and someone who is not able to discover the real truth beyond the surface of the world. The next affair with the Dutch girl Magdelein proves to be too tight for him because he is basically suffocated by her love. Mugezi has to struggle with the female principle in his life. As I have already mentioned, having no 'real' mother, he was seeking for the part of his identity which had been spoilt by Padlock, his 'mother.' His longing for the life he was born into, in a rural village under his great aunt's tutelage, could not draw him back to an Africa irreparably damaged by colonial racism.

---

[201] Jaggi, <http://www.booksunlimited.co.uk/reviews/generalfiction/0,6121,399107,00.htm>.

Serenity tries to spot his crimes by "writing down his exploits in a story that took place in the legendary land of Abyssinia, changing the name of the characters..." (Isegawa 440) He is estranged from what is going on in his country and he can only "marvel at the way history wrote, erased and rewrote itself." (Isegawa 441) Serenity and Mugezi, as well as Padlock and all the others, undertake a hard struggle to recover their inner-selves. The war destroyed their already split personality and left them with nothing but the wreckages of the aftermath. The last section of the book describes both Padlock and Serenity's death. Padlock is gored by a bull and tossed "like a Korean trapeze artist...Falling and screaming, she landed with both shoulders on the gigantic marmorean horns, feet in the air like St. Peter on the cross...She was back in the clouds, headed for Rome and the Holy Land." (Isegawa 447) Thus, Serenity's world narrowed down to the simple things because he realizes that in his whole life he resisted the "miracle-working demons of religion." (Isegawa 450) One day, as he is walking around the lake, he is attacked and killed by a crocodile. "In that final instant, he suddenly realised where his wife's bones lay, but because the ancient art of communicating with the dead through dreams had been killed off in the family by Catholicism, Western education and abject neglect, Serenity's knowledge did not leave the belly of the crocodile, not even when it died ten years after." (Isegawa 452)

After splitting up with his Dutch girlfriend, Mugezi is about to leave for Amsterdam. He sits in front of Central station and

> as I looked, my head began to spin: I was getting dizzy. People seemed to be walking upside down, the dead rising from their graves, the living diving into fresh graves...The mixing and juxtaposition of peoples became mind-blowing, the destinations and points of departure mythic. I held on to the cement bank in order to stop myself from spewing or getting spewed...I was back in my element: watching, planning, waiting for the right time to strike. Abyssinia was on my mind; so was my new foothold on this precipitous hilltop. It has always been a Herculean task for Abyssinians to get their foot in the door, but once in, they never budge. I was in. (Isegawa 462)

Almost all the nation's potential and hope was crushed during Amin's brutal misrule (1971-1979). Obote II saw minimal improvements, culminating in an overthrow in 1985. Yoweri Museveni, who has held power since 1986, made many changes for the better but runs a one-party state and has in recent years involved Uganda in the senseless and wasteful conflict in what used to be Zaire. In addition, Uganda was among the first and hardest hit countries to face Aids in the 1980's.

VI. Conclusion

"Not all peoples can be colonised; only those who experience this need [for dependency]"…the coming of the Europeans "…was unconsciously expected, even desired, by the future subject peoples."[202] This seems to explain the superiority complex of the white race and the inferiority complex of the black men, which resulted in asking themselves whether they were men at all. Thus, the black man began to "suffer from not being a white to the degree that the white man imposes discrimination on me, makes me a colonised native, robs me of all worth, all individuality, tells me that I am a parasite on the world, that I must bring myself as quickly as possible into step with the white world…"[203] The imperialistic white world, the world of Joseph Conrad and the Victorians at the turn of the century grew into a mighty empire that visualised the conquest and the domination of the rest of the world as one of its main targets. They felt superior and considered the 'others' to be different and animal-like, and therefore, simple brutes. Throughout the centuries the black race has been subjected to racism, prejudices and violence on a scale not to be explained and comprehended. Thus, it is a demanding task for them to come to terms with their past; even more challenging is the attempt to free themselves from discrimination and the dominating white world which invaded the African continent like 'locusts' and basically 'ate' up black existence: it is the white Europeans that have been the parasites.

Joseph Conrad, Chinua Achebe and Moses Isegawa depict the African continent at three different stages of history, namely, the end of the 19th century when the Belgians under King Leopold II invaded the Congo Free State; the first half of the 20th century when the British missionaries 'civilised' the Igbos in Nigeria and therefore, spoilt their rich cultural heritage; and the second half of the 20th century, precisely from 1960 to 1980, when Uganda was psychologically and physically exploited by political tyranny during post-independence. Furthermore, the all have been written under different circumstances: *Heart of Darkness* was written at the end of the 19th century and reflects Victorianism and its mode of thinking about racism and the superiority of the white race; *Things Fall Apart* was published in 1958 and

---

[202] Mannoni, *Prospero and Caliban: The Psychology of Colonization* 85-86.
[203] Fanon, *Black Skin, White Masks* 98.

reflects the experience of the Igbos as they were flooded by the white missionaries; *Abyssinian Chronicles* was published in 2000 and represents the attempt of the Ugandan population to deal with their loss of identity and the wreckages of post-colonialism. They all three deal with the impact of the colonial enterprise on the African continent, but from three different perspectives: the coloniser's, Joseph Conrad through the use of Marlow; the colonised's, Chinua Achebe with Okonkwo; and the decolonised's, Moses Isegawa with Mugezi. As a matter of fact, the history of each of the countries, Congo, Nigeria and Uganda strongly influenced the authors when writing their books. **Joseph Conrad** describes the invasion of the Congo Free State by the Belgians from the coloniser's point of view. The reader is confronted with the atrocities of the imperial 'machinery' in the colonies and is appalled at the hollowness of the 'death march' of the Europeans. Conrad creates Kurtz, Marlow, and the 'pilgrims' as the representatives of the colonial regime and the body of the 'Metropolis,' who invade the dark continent to civilise the 'cannibals.' Quite contrarily, the author depicts the natives of the Congo as mysterious, genuine and as the antagonistic force to the white missionaries. Moreover, Conrad concludes that the colonisers are hollow at the core; Kurtz came to the Congo with moral ideas because he wanted to bring the light of civilization to the native people, but when he got in contact with nature and realised the dishonesty and corruption of the Western world, he lost his sanity. Marlow is allowed to get a glimpse of truth and comes to the conclusion that the 'modern' human beings are not ready to accept reality, but actually they live with the lie of civilisation that prevents them from madness. The women in the story are out of touch with reality and ignorant of their own futile existence. Nevertheless, the female element proves to be decisive for the two opposing forces nature and human civilization.

Chinua Achebe gives us a detailed description of Nigeria before the arrival of the white missionaries and the District Commissioners from the colonised's point of view. He introduces the traditional life of the Igbos and their customs and stresses the fact that there had been a culture before the white missionaries saw it as their duty to civilise it. Achebe describes the economic life of the tribe without forgetting to point at the cultural richness within the African people. The colonial impact at the fringe is effectively portrayed as the 'Second Coming' that has as its result the annihilation of the old order and the formation of new European values. Once again, femininity seems to be the powerful source behind the order of the world, which keeps it in balance. By ignoring the controlling cause Okonkwo is doomed to die in his attempt to fight back to the empire. The coloniser is seen as someone who appeals to the outcasts and weak in order to undermine the native tribe and its rules. Achebe reveals how the natives were forced to accept the aggressor's culture and government; furthermore, the past of the black continent was reduced to an irrelevant chapter in the book of imperialism.

Moses Isegawa tries to face up to the past of Uganda after independence from the decolonised's point of view. His main protagonist Mugezi is confronted with the wreckages of imperialism and the new situation of independence. After describing ordinary life in the country he switches to life in the city under the horrifying regime of Idi Amin. While he and the other members of his family are searching for a new identity, they are trapped in the aftermath of the colonial past. Loss of self-confidence and respect initially prevent them from redefining blackness but the ultimate return 'back to the Metropolis' signals an original step into the direction of self-fulfilment. The role of the women is decisive for the development of the story as femininity stands for identity and personality; having been deprived of one's identity means regaining one's sense of individuality. Religion and the female element help the protagonists to seek a way to learn from the ravages of time.

The novels depict Africa in three different ways because, as I have already mentioned, the authors portray Africa at three different stages of history. Joseph Conrad portrayed Africa as the antithesis to Europe, and simultaneously, developed different characters that functioned as opposing forces representing African and European culture and mentality. The Victorian writer defined Africa as a mysterious place, unknown, amorphous, and dangerous whereas Europe was depicted as being civilised, noble, and mighty. The Europeans' duty was to leave their mother country and to civilise their opponents, who were uncivilised and ready to accept the European culture and rules. Africa was not considered to be a country with a rich cultural heritage because it was simply ignored that there had been a 'life' without the Europeans. Conrad drew a picture of Africa that makes the reader realise that Africa was an unknown country for the Europeans and the rest of the world, but therefore was genuine, rich and innocent. Imperialism and colonialism totally ignored their existing culture and systematically destroyed it; at the same time the 'missionaries' proved the ignorance and nullity of their own mother country characterised by hollowness and avarice. Chinua Achebe, on the contrary, presents Africa as a place with a rich culture relying on oral tradition. He introduces many proverbs and stories, and thoroughly describes the African reality before the arrival of the missionaries.

The reader is confronted with an Africa that was 'blossoming' before the invasion because it was a different culture with various rules and habits. One realises the existence of a culture and the existence of an opposition towards the European invasion, but simultaneously one also recognizes how the African reality was flooded by the eurocentric worldview. The Igbos were undermined in their authority, and as a consequence, they doubted their own way of life; generally speaking, they were assimilated and convinced of the authenticity of the European values and morals. Needless to say, the Ibos partly drove themselves and particularly others into the hands of the missionaries as the story of Okonkwo and his son Nwoye shows. The failure to recognize the principle of love and femininity, mercy and trust brought about the annihilation of the African past. Moses Isegawa portrays the 'recent' history of Uganda as he writes about the country's independence and aftermath of the colonial domination. Like China Achebe he tries to convey the sense of naturalness of Uganda, and its decisive role within the African continent. Isegawa observes Africa from a 'modern' point of view as he highlights the horrendous condition of the country after the independence; moreover, his novel tells the reader of the 20th century and one of its most dreadful viruses, namely AIDS. The author's main attempt is to demonstrate Africa's position during the postcolonial period and its people's effort to come to terms with their past and future. The Africans and especially the people from Uganda are searching for a new identity and therefore, leave their home country to return to the 'metropolis.' They try to face their inferiority complex and to demonstrate to the white world that blackness has been a decisive factor in the development of history. Africa is a country with many problems and risks but has a certain fascination that stems from the magical elements, which characterise African history.

As far as language and style are concerned, the three novels reveal an interesting picture. Joseph Conrad uses a narrative within a narrative in order to stress the gap between narration and reality within the story. He introduces an omniscient narrator who interrupts the flow of the story from time to time. Chinua Achebe and Moses Isegawa have an omniscient narrator as well, who embodies the central figure of the narrative. Thus, Conrad uses the so-called 'delayed decoding', which enforces the dream-like quality of the journey and the book as a whole. *Heart of Darkness* reflects Victorianism and the general attitude of Conrad's time and therefore, it is not a surprise that he uses words like 'Nigger' and other derogative terms for the black population. Nevertheless, Achebe accuses him of being a racist for the fact that he does not grant speech to the natives in the jungle, and generally speaking, he pictures the African and especially the Congolese people as being cannibals, devil-like and inferior. Conrad outlines Africa at the turn of the 19th century and reproduces what he saw. Kurtz basically embodies Conrad as far as the journey to the Congo is concerned, because both left Europe with some moral ideas but were utterly disappointed when they realised the failure of their mission. He wrote down the experiences of his trip up the Congo River and equipped it with a symbolic meaning; he even admitted having made Kurtz too symbolic at all. Nevertheless, he wanted to highlight the hollowness of European society and imperialism, and for that reason, he used the mode of thinking and the ideas of that time.

Chinua Achebe's *Things Fall Apart* was published in 1958 and it marked a new era: in order to reach most of the people all over the world, he uses the English language; different 'englishes' were created. Moses Isegawa follows that tradition when *Abyssinian Chronicles* was published in 2000. In *Things Fall Apart* Achebe describes the traditional life of the Igbos and in doing so, he uses a lot of proverbs, code-switching and untranslated words. These means of narration stress the 'otherness' of the African culture but at the same time combine it with 'english.' The untranslated words and the proverbs are characteristic of the oral tradition and prove the existence of a highly developed culture long before the arrival of the Europeans. Themes such as religion and femininity seem to be decisive for the development of the story. Especially the female figure conditions the fate of the protagonist as the female vein is the all-transcending force behind nature. Moreover, the various gods and customs enrich the colour of the book. Achebe portrays the arrival of the white missionaries with their language and style; as a result, a new language and style has to be created after it has been ignored and destroyed. Moses Isegawa goes on celebrating that kind of creation when he uses his 'english' to describe the situation in Uganda after independence. Like Achebe forty years before, Isegawa makes use of the oral tradition to underline the African character of the story. Untranslated words, code-switching and magical elements seem to draw up the colonial experience. The book has been compared to Salman Rushdie's *Midnight's Children* because of the use of elements of 'magic realism' such as the death of Mugezi's parents when she is killed by a bull and he is eaten by a crocodile. Isegawa succeeds in presenting Uganda's fate from independence to 1980, and that of the colonised people together with their search for their lost identity. The amalgamation of traditional elements and 'english' reveals the importance of religion and the female dimension for the protagonists as their revenge on the white man consists of being with a white woman; thus, the Africans look for their lost female dimension. Going back to the imperial 'Metropolis' means not forgetting one's roots but creating something new based on the past.

The imperialistic coloniser imported capitalism and exploitation from the European city and was of the opinion that it was his duty to civilise the fiend-like cannibals. As a matter of fact, the colonised were a developed and intelligent 'race' whereas the Europeans were ignorant when they thought that "the Negro is an animal, the Negro is bad, the Negro is mean, the Negro is ugly..."[204] The dominated colonised have redefined blackness and have created an original way of spreading the 'otherness' but an 'otherness' that is based on equality and respect. According to Sir Alan Burns "colour is the most obvious outward manifestation of race that has been made the criterion by which men are judged, irrespective of their social or educational attainments. The light-skinned races have come to despise all those of a darker colour, and the dark-skinned peoples will no longer accept without protest the inferior position to which they have been relegated." (Sir Alan Burns quoted in Fanon: 1967, 118) Colonialism spoilt the sense of uniqueness and individuality of the African peoples, and independence meant the redefinition of values and the return to the 'Metropolis' to prove that the African tradition was based on

> Order-Earnestness-Poetry and Freedom. From the untroubled private citizen to the almost fabulous leader there was an unbroken chain of understanding and trust. No science? Indeed yes; but also, to protect them from fear, they possessed great myths in which the most subtle observation and the most daring imagination were balanced and blended. No art? They had their magnificent sculpture, in which human feeling erupted so unrestrained yet always followed the obsessive laws of rhythm in its organisation of its major elements of a material called upon to capture, in order to redistribute, the most secret forces of the universe...
> (Aimé Césaire quoted in Fanon: 1967, 131)

Joseph Conrad, Chinua Achebe, and Moses Isegawa effectively describe the African transition from domination by the colonial masters to the act of writing back to the centre as a redefinition of black identity.

---

[204] Fanon, *Black Skin, White Masks* 113.

Bibliography

Primary Sources:

Achebe, Chinua. *Things Fall Apart*. Oxford: Heinemann, 1958.

Conrad, Joseph. *Heart of Darkness*. London: Penguin Books, 1902.

Isegawa, Moses. *Abyssinian Chronicles*. New York: Alfred A. Knopf, 2000.

Texts and Criticism:

"Abyssinian Chronicles." *The Borzoi Reader* Summer 2000. 2 February 2001
    <http://www.randomhouse.com/knopf/borzoi/2000summer/isegawa.htm>.

Abiola, Irele. *Introduction to African Literature: An Anthology of Critical Writing*. Ed. Ulli Beier.
    London: Longman, 1967.

Achebe, Chinua. "An Image of Africa." *The Massachusetts Review* 18 (1977): 782-94.

---."An Image of Africa: Racism in Conrad's *Heart of Darkness*." *Joseph Conrad,*
    'Heart of Darkness.' Ed. Robert Kimbrough. 3rd ed. New York: Norton, 1988. 251-262.

---.*The Trouble with Nigeria*. Oxford: Heinemann Educational Publishers, 1983.

---."Where Angels Fear to Tread." *Nigeria Magazine* 75 (1962): 61-2.

Adelmann, Gary. *'Heart of Darkness': Search for the Unconscious*. Boston: Twayne Publishers,
    1987.

African-English Literature: A Short Survey and Anthology of Prose and Poetry up to 1965. Ed.
    Anne Tibble. London: Peter Owen, 1965.

Ambrosini, Richard. *Conrad's Fiction as Critical Discourse*. Cambridge: Cambridge UP, 1991.

Ashcroft, Bill, Gareth Griffiths, and Helen Tiffin. *The Empire Writes Back. Theory and Practice in Post-Colonial Literatures*. London and New York: Routledge, 1989.

Awoonor, Koofi. *The Breast of the Earth*. New York: Anchor Press, 1976.

Baines, Jocelyn. *Joseph Conrad: A Critical Biography*. London: Weidenfeld & Nicholson, 1960.

Baker, Robert. "Watt's Conrad." *Contemporary Literature* 22 (1981): 116-126.

Berman, Jeffrey. *Joseph Conrad: Writing as Rescue*. New York: Astra Books, 1977.

Betts, Raymond F. *Decolonisation*. London and New York: Routledge, 1998.

Bivona, Daniel. *British Imperial Literature, 1870-1940. Writing and the Administration of Empire*. Cambridge: Cambridge UP, 1998.

Blant, J.M. *The Colonizer's Model of the World: Geographical Diffusionism and Eurocentric History*. New York: The Guildford Press, 1993.

Boehmer, Elleke. *Colonial and Postcolonial Literature. Migrant Metaphors*. Oxford: Oxford UP, 1995.

Brantlinger, Patrick. "*Heart of Darkness*: Anti-Imperialism, Racism, or Impressionism?" *Case Studies in Contemporary Criticism. 'Heart of Darkness': Joseph Conrad*. Ed. Ross C. Murfin. 2nd ed. Boston: Bedford, 1996. 277-96.

---.*Rule of Darkness: British Literature and Imperialism, 1830-1914*. Ithaca: Cornell UP, 1988.

Brook, Thomas. "Preserving and Keeping Order by Killing Time in *Heart of Darkness*." *Case Studies in Contemporary Criticism. Joseph Conrad: 'Heart of Darkness.'* Ed. Ross C. Murfin. 2nd ed. Boston: Bedford, 1996. 239-57.

Brown, Lloyd W. "Cultural Norms and Modes of Perception in Achebe's Fiction." *Critical Perspectives on Nigerian Literatures*. Ed. Bernth Lindfors. Washington: Three Continent Press, 1976. 131-45.

Carroll, David. *Chinua Achebe: Novelist, Poetic, Critic*. London: Macmillan, 1980.

"Complete Review." *The Borzoi Reader* Summer 2000. 2 February 2001 <http://www.complete.review.com/reviews/uganda/isegawa.htm>.

Conrad, Joseph. "Geography and Some Explorers." *Tales of Hearsay and Last Essays*. Ed. Richard Curle. London: J.M. Dent, 1926. 10-17.

---. *A Personal Record*. London: J.M. Dent & Sons, 1912.

---. "The Congo Diary." *Tales of Hearsay and Last Essays*. London: J.M. Dent & Sons, 1955. 7-16.

---. "The Preface (1897)." *The Nigger of the Narcissus*. New York: Norton, 1979. 145-48.

---. "Well Done." *Notes on Life and Letters*. London: J.M. Dent & Sons, 1921. 189-91.

---. *The Collected Letters of Joseph Conrad, Volume I/II, 1861-1897*. Eds. Frederick R. Karl and Laurence Davies. Cambridge: Cambridge UP, 1983.

---. *Congo Diary and Other Uncollected Pieces*. Ed. Zdzislaw Najder. New York: Doubleday, 1978.

Conrad's Polish Background. Ed. Zdzislaw Najder. Oxford: Oxford UP, 1964.

Cook, Mercer, and Stephen E. Henderson. *African Voices of Protest: Militant Black Writer in Africa and the United States.* Wisconsin: Madison, 1969.

Cox, C.B. *Joseph Conrad: The Modern Imagination.* London: J.M. Dent & Sons, 1974.

Deuby, David. "Jungle Fever." *New Yorker* (Nov.6 1995): 118-129.

Dobrinsky, Joseph. *The Artist in Conrad's Fiction: A Psychocritical Study.* London: UMI, 1989.

Dorall, E.N. "Conrad and Coppola: Different Centres of Darkness." *Southeast Asian Review of English* 1 (1980): 19-27.

Emenyonu, Ernest N. *The Rise of the Ibo Novel.* Oxford: Oxford UP, 1978.

Fanon, Frantz. *Black Skin, White Masks.* Trans. Charles Lam Markmann. New York: Groove Press, 1967.

---.*The Wretched of the Earth.* London: Penguin Books, 1963.

---.*Critical Perspectives.* Ed. Anthony C. Alessandrini. London and New York: Routledge, 1999.

Firchow, Peter Edgerly. *Envisioning Africa: Racism and Imperialism in Conrad's 'Heart of Darkness.'* Kentucky: Kentucky UP, 2000.

Fleischman, Avrom. *Conrad's Politics: Community and Anarchy in the Fiction of Joseph Conrad.* Baltimore: Johns Hopkins, 1967.

Frazer, Sir George James. *The Golden Bough.* New York: Macmillan, 1960.

Gillon, Adam. *Joseph Conrad. Twayne's English Authors Series.* Ed. Kinley E. Roby. Boston: Twayne Publishers, 1982.

Glave, E.J. "Cruelty in the Congo Free State." *Century Magazine* 54 (1897): 699-715.

Goonetilleke, D.C.R.A. *Joseph Conrad: Beyond Culture and Background*. London: Macmillan, 1990.

Gray, Paul. "Coming of Age in Chaos." *Time Europe* 156 May 2000. 2 February 2001 <http://www.time.com/time/europe/magazine/2000/0731/gray.htm>.

Guerard, Albert J. "The Journey Within." *Conrad: 'Heart of Darkness,' 'Nostromo' and 'Under Western Eyes.' A Casebook*. Ed. C.B. Cox. London: Macmillan, 1981. 49-62.

Guetti, James. "The Failure of the Imagination, 1965." *Conrad: 'Heart of Darkness,' 'Nostromo' and 'Under Western Eyes.' A Casebook*. Ed. C.B. Cox. London: Macmillan, 1981. 65-77.

Hagen, William M. "*Heart of Darkness* and the Process of Apocalypse Now." *Conradiana* 13 (1981): 45-54.

'Heart of Darkness': Joseph Conrad. Ed. D.C.R.A. Goonetilleke. London: Broadview Literary Books, 1995.

Hennessy, Maurice N. "The Congo Free State: A Brief History, 1876 to 1908." *Congo*. London: Pall Mall Press, 1961. 13-27.

Isichei, Elisabeth. *The Ibo People and the Europeans: The Genesis of a Relationship to 1906*. London: Faber and Faber, 1973.

Jaggi, Maya. "Into the Heart of Grunge." *The Guardian* November 18 2000. 2 February 2001 <http://www.booksunlimited.co.uk/reviews/generalfiction/0,6121,399107,00.htm>.

Karl, Frederick R. "Introduction to the *Danse Macabre*: Conrad's *Heart of Darkness*." *'Heart of Darkness': Joseph Conrad, A Case Study in Contemporary Criticism*. Ed. Ross C. Murfin. New York: St. Martin's Press, 1989. 123-136.

Kemoli, Arthur. *An H.E.B. Student's Guide: Notes on Chinua Achebe's 'Things Fall Apart.'* Nairobi: Heinemann, 1975.

Killam, G.D. *The Writings of Chinua Achebe*. London: Heinemann, 1969.

Kimbrough, Robert. *The World's Classics: Conrad, Joseph. 'Youth,' 'Heart of Darkness,' 'The End of the Tether.'* Ed. and Intro. Robert Kimbrough. Oxford: Oxford UP, 1984.

Kipling, Rudyard. *White Man's Burden*, 1899.

Kortenaar, Neil Ten. "How the Centre is Made To Hold in *Things Fall Apart*." *Postcolonial Literatures: Achebe, Ngugi, Desai, Walcott*. Eds. Michael Parker and Roger Starkey. New York: St. Martin's, 1995. 31-51.

Lawrence, Margaret. *Long Drums and Cannons: Nigerian Dramatists and Novelists 1952-1966*. London: Macmillan, 1968.

Lindfors, Bernth. "The Palm Oil with which Achebe's Words Are Eaten." *African Literature Today* 1 (1968): 3-18.

Loomba, Ania. *Colonialism/Postcolonialism*. London and New York: Routledge, 1998.

Mahood, M.M. *The Colonial Encounter: A Reading of Six Novels*. London: Rex Collings, 1977.

Mannoni, Dominique O. *Prospero and Caliban: The Psychology of Colonization*. Trans. Pamela Powesland. London: Heinemann, 1956.

McLauchlan, Juliet. "The 'Value' and 'Significance' of *Heart of Darkness.*" *Conradiana* 15 (1983): 3-21.

Miller, J. Hillis. *Poets of Reality: Six Twentieth Century Writers*. Cambridge: Harvard University Press, 1966.

Morty, Ali G. "Review of *Things Fall Apart.*" *Black Orpheus* 6 (1959): 48-50.

Moser, Thomas. *Joseph Conrad: Achievement and Decline*. Cambridge: Harvard UP, 1957.

Ngugi Wa Thiong'o. *Homecoming: Essays on African and Caribbean Literature, Culture and Politics*. London: Heinemann, 1972.

---.*Decolonising the Mind. The Politics of Language in African Literature*. London: James Currey, 1986.

Njoku, Benedict Chiaka. *The Four Novels of Chinua Achebe: A Critical Study, American University Studies*. New York: Peter Lang, 1984.

Ogu, Julius N. "The Concept of Madness in Chinua Achebe's Writings." *Journal of Commonwealth Literature* 18.1 (1983): 48-54.

Ojinmah, Umelo. *Chinua Achebe: New Perspectives*. Nigeria: Spectrum Books Limited, 1991.

Omava-Otunnu, Amii. *Politics and the Military in Uganda, 1890-1985*. London: Macmillan, 1987.

Omenka, Nicholas Ibeawuchi. *The School in the Service of Evangelisation: The Catholic Educational Impact in Eastern Nigeria 1886-1950. Studies on Religion in Africa VI*. Leiden: E.J. Brill, 1989.

Palmer, Eustace. *An Introduction to the African Novel*. London: Heinemann, 1972.

Patterson, Christina. "Amin was his Saviour. Until Reality Set In." *The Guardian* November 12 2000. 2 February 2001 <http://www.booksunlimited.co.uk/Print/0,3858,4089735,00.htm>.

Pennycock, Alastair. *English and the Discourses of Colonialism*. London: Routledge, 1998.

Phillips, Jerry. "Cannibalism qua capitalism: the Metaphorics of Accumulation in Marx, Conrad, Shakespeare, and Marlow." *Cannibalism and the Colonial World*. Eds. Francis Baker, Peter Hulme, and Margaret Iversen. Cambridge: Cambridge UP, 1998. 183-203.

Price, Jim. "Isegawa Chronicles Pain, Passions of Central Africa." *Milwaukee Journal Sentinel* June 16 2000. 2 February 2001 <http://www.jsonline.com/entbooks/reviews/jun00/bk.abyss18061600as.htm>.

Ravenscroft, Arthur. *Chinua Achebe*. Ed. Ian Scott-Kilvert. London: Longman, Green & Co, 1969.

Reid, Stephen A. "The 'Unspeakable Rites' in *Heart of Darkness*." *Conrad: A Collection of Critical Essays. Twentieth Century Views*. Ed. Marvin Mudrick. New Jersey: Prentice-Hall, 1966. 45-54.

Rushdie, Salman. *Imaginary Homelands: Essays and Criticism 1981-1991*. London: Granta, 1991.

Said, Edward W. *Orientalism*. New York: Vintage Books, 1978.

Sarvan, C.P. "Racism and the *Heart of Darkness*." *The International Fiction Review* 7 (1980): 6-10.

Saveson, John E. "Conrad's View of Primitive Peoples in *Lord Jim* and *Heart of Darkness*." *Modern Fiction Studies* 16 (1970): 174-5.

Schweitzer, Albert. *On the Edge of the Primeval Forest*. Trans. C.T. Campion. London: A. and C. Black, 1924.

Simmons, Arthur. *Notes on Joseph Conrad: With some Unpublished Letters*. London: Arthur Simmons and Meyers & Co., 1925.

Singh, Frances B. "The Colonialist Bias of *Heart of Darkness*." *Conradiana* 10 (1978): 41-54.

Speed, Diana. "Review of *Things Fall Apart*." *Black Orpheus* 5 (1959): 52.

Stock, A.G. "Yeats and Achebe." *Journal of Commonwealth Literature* 5 (1968): 105-111.

Trilling, Lionel. *Beyond Culture*. London: Secker and Warburg, 1966.

Walsh, William. *A Manifold Voice: Studies in Commonwealth Literature*. London: Chatto and Windus, 1970.

Wassermann, Jerry. "Narrative Presence: The Illusion of Language in *Heart of Darkness*." *Critical Essays on Joseph Conrad*. Boston: G.K. Hall & Co, 1987. 102-112.

Watt, Cedric. "*Heart of Darkness*." *The Cambridge Companion to Joseph Conrad*. Ed. J.H. Stape. Cambridge: Cambridge UP, 1996. Chapter 3.

Watt, Ian. *Conrad in the 19th Century*. Berkeley: California UP, 1979.

---. "Impressionism and Symbolism in *Heart of Darkness*." *Conrad in the Nineteenth Century*. Berkeley and Los Angeles: California UP, 1979. 168-200, 249-53.